TRENDS AND IMPACT OF INFORMATION TECHNOLOGY IN LIBRARIES
A Quality Paradigm of Excellence

TRENDS AND IMPACT OF INFORMATION TECHNOLOGY IN LIBRARIES

A Quality Paradigm of Excellence

By

Ashok Kumar Sahu

Rabindra Kumar Mahapatra

Ess Ess Publications

New Delhi

TRENDS AND IMPACT OF INFORMATION TECHNOLOGY IN LIBRARIES
A Quality Paradigm of Excellence

ISBN: 978-81-7000-816-3

First Published 2016

Published by:
Ess Ess Publications
4831/24, Ansari Road,
Darya Ganj,
New Delhi-110 002.
INDIA
Phones: 23260807, 41563444
Fax: 41563334
E-mail: info@essessreference.com
www.essessreference.com

Cover Design by *Patch Creative Unit*

Printed and bound in India at Salasar Imaging Systems.

Contents

Acknowledgements

Preface

1 Information Technology 1

2 Information Technology in Libraries 28

3 Impact of Information Technology in Libraries 68

4 Networking of Libraries in India 102

5 Trends of Information Technology in Libraries 124

Acknowledgements

First and foremost, I would like to thank my guide, family, and parents for their guidance and constant support to complete this book. I am also very grateful to my Ph.D. guide and co-author Dr.Rabindra Kumar Mahapatra for his insights and innovative ideas from time to time at all stage of the work.

I would also express my gratitude to Dr.M.D.Patra, Executive Director, and Mr.B.M.Misra, Principal Adviser-DEPR, Reserve Bank of India for their support, encouragement and permission to publish this book. My grateful acknowledge to my all colleagues of Central Library, Reserve Bank of India for their support.

My sincere regards to my beloved parents, family members (Sujata, Suhani & Swastik) and In-Laws, whose inspiration and whishes led me to the completion of this work.

My sincere thanks to all who helped to typing and bearing inconvenience on account of working long hours for preparing this book. Last but not the least, I thank to Mr.Sumit Sethi, Managing Director, Ess Ess Publications, New Delhi who has taken lots of pain to publish this book.

— **Ashok Kumar Sahu**

Preface

The rapid advances in information technologies combined with accelerating developments in computer technology have offered tremendous opportunities in the field of information management. The developments in information technology have made us possible to access a wide variety of electronic information resources across the globe easily, instantaneously and economically. Worldwide libraries have been exploring new technologies for providing better and faster access to vast information resources and effective value added information services to their users. Information Technology has proved as better solutions to achieve greater level of efficiency, productivity and excellence services in libraries. It has also widened the scope of the five laws of Library and Information Science, Thanks to the sagacious personality Dr. S. R. Ranganathan. The application and accessibility to IT facilitates, the free flow of information, creative expression, effective management, etc. are the major issues forced the libraries to adopt Information Technology and the challenges are still ahead.

Application of IT in libraries has become inevitable in an era of information explosion and widespread use of digital information resources. Effective application of IT in libraries helps in performing their operations and services most efficiently. Over the last two decades, libraries have witnessed the impact of information technology on the structure of services. Many libraries are already using computers and advanced systems and many more are currently implementing such systems. The Library staff plays the key role in making the library resource available to the users. The effectiveness of any library depends on the quality and quantity of the personnel. It is necessary that the staff provided in the libraries should be properly trained and qualified. In Service training for the library professionals to be promoted to increase efficiency and effectiveness in library services in the new automated library environment. In the absence of strong telecommunication channels, the Internet facility is yet to find its success. Financial constraints are the major hindrance for the growth at national, local and organizational levels. As a result the implementation of IT facilities for libraries are not receiving adequate support from their parent body. Majority of libraries do not have computer facilities. The print media is still a major source of information in libraries. The libraries will continue to suffer if they cannot find a mechanism to acquire IT. The authorities should realise the need of this vital change and start turning to the present day requirements.

As the pace of technological change accelerated and expectations of services increased, it became apparent that change would be a constant, but often unpredictable, factor in the library and information environment. The Library authorities have already recognized and realised that an appropriate framework in which to manage constant change in all aspects of the library management would be critical to future success and sustainability in an increasingly competitive environment, with wealthy, century's old, metropolitan libraries. The past two decades have seen a great deal of change due to IT resulting in a demand for new patterns of scholarly information. These technological advancements have made significant impact on the growth of knowledge and unlocking of human potential. In library environment, the impact is clearly visible on information resources, services, and people.

The impact of information technology is enormous and global in its magnitude. It has become an integral part of all aspects of the library. It has a profound impact on library operations, information resources &, services, staff skills requirements and users expectations. Information Technology has virtually unlimited potential for variety if useful applications in libraries as it significantly contributes to the improved quality, increased productivity, more efficient operations, better resource sharing and more effective services to the users. The proper exploration of new technologies in library is no longer a matter of choice but a matter of survival in an era of rapidly changing technology and global knowledge society. Today the success of a modern library is increasingly dependent on the most effective utilization and strategic management of new technologies in libraries. Excellent service, it is believed that it requires excellent people and high quality, cost-effective supporting processes and they are not only essential to the success of the researchers and students of organization, but are of strategic importance in achieving the organization's mission and goals. In adopting the excellence framework, the libraries not only sought to improve their performance in all areas but to measure and compare performance and outcomes.

This book helps the library professionals to better understand how to implement information technology with appropriate planning. The book would be a valuable resource for the librarians, academics, professionals, students and researchers for their research work. It would be useful to provide a broad and a clear idea about the computerization of the libraries and thus help to design appropriate strategic plans for an effective implementation of IT in libraries and also to provide a clear insight about the benefits of using IT to library professionals. The study contributes towards those libraries, which are seriously interested to computerize their libraries and with a commitment to provide quality library services to their users.

— Ashok Kumar Sahu

these technologies to fulfill three objectives:

1. Increase Networking Opportunities : helps to connect universities as well as individuals within those to one another. This ability to network is especially important for students in rural areas and students in developing countries.

2. Provide Distance Learning : learning has become Web-based, as a result, IT have started to replace correspondence courses.

3. Supplement Traditional Learning : One of the most common uses in education involves students using software programs like Microsoft Word to produce otherwise traditional written assignments.

Rapid advances in information technology combined with accelerating developments in computer technology have offered tremendous opportunities in the field of information management. Developments in information technology have made possible to access a wide variety of electronic information resources across the globe easily, instantaneously and economically. Computers are used for generation, processing and storage of information and IT has made the information more meaningful, useful and easily accessible remotely, in transferring information with the help of telecommunication and data communications. Telecommunication made possible in facilitating in transferring information via telephone, fax, telegraph, radio or television, either directly or via computer whereas Communication system the transmitters, a channels and a receivers allow to transmit information from transmitter to receiver through a channel. Rowley (1993), the essential components of a communication are a transmitter to send information, and receiver to accept it, a transmission medium/channel through which the message travels, signals and codes which represent message, and network controls to ensure that the message gets to its destination.

Viswanathan (1995) stated that the communication

systems are classified according to the channel used into radio, microwave, satellite, and co-axial cable and fiber optic communications. Developments in IT have greatly changed the methods of information handling. IT is combination of tools and procedures that facilitate the generation, acquisition, storage, organization, retrieval, searching, viewing, updating and transmission of information using electronic means. IT includes the tools like computer programs, databases, communication networks, analysis and design methods, programming languages, artificial intelligence, knowledge base, etc. It provides opportunities for libraries and information centres to widen of their resources and services and to increase their significance within the organization it serve. Library and information centres have been employing IT and its facilities and features, the electronic information resources and services to satisfy the diverse information needs of the users. E-journals, CD-ROM databases, online databases, e-books, web-based resources, and other electronic media are fast replacing the traditional resources of libraries (Haneefa, 2007).

Access to information is not a new phenomenon but it exists through ages. Libraries' being the centre of information storage and retrieval exists since from ancient times in one form or the other. The libraries have transformed from museums to digital libraries over the time due to intervention and adoption of various technologies. The invention of ink, paper, printing technology and information technologies are the major technological milestones in the history of library transformation. The printing technology helped the mass production of books and other printed materials and brought them to the portals of the library as primary storage media. As science & technology advanced, the print media have been augmented by non-print media such as microfilms, audio-visual aids, magnetic tapes and CD-ROMs as the medium of information storage and retrieval. Since 1950s the developments in IT induced libraries from museums to traditional libraries and transform to digital libraries incorporating documents available in electronic formats.

Information technology has emerged as the most potent tool to collect, organize and disseminate information to the people at large scale through communication networks. It is one of the fastest spreading technologies in the world in terms of use and production. It is diffusing rapidly into all industrial and service sectors and is seen as one of the most crucial technologies affecting economic growth in developing countries. Its use is ubiquitous in the industrialized countries to the extent that in United States investment in IT accounts for about 50% of total new capital investment by corporations. The production of IT products and services is a major industry in the US, Japan and Europe. Several newly industrialized countries, such as China, Korea, Taiwan, Singapore and Brazil have become significant producers and users of IT.

Invention of computer is a great contribution to libraries and its introduction was traced in early 80's in libraries. It has transformed almost every aspect of how the library provides its services and performs its work behind the scenes. This resulted in automation of library in-house operations, Online Public Access Catalogue (OPAC), remote access, digitization, and creation of digital libraries. The issues related to current technology discussed and addressed by the present day libraries are:

i. Digitization of special collections, establishing institutional depositories,

ii. Use of automated electronic collection management software,

iii. Implementation of wireless and mobile technologies for all time remote/campus wide access,

iv. Bar-coded library transactions,

v. CD mirror servers and accessing CDs available on network;

vi. Application of RFID in Library security systems,

vii. Web site development, web-programming and management, integration of web OPAC and integration of multi-language on single platform,

viii. Production and Use of e-books and e-journals,

ix. Services for distance learning students, physically challenged

x. Technology education, training and instructional/ education technology to support teaching and learning

xi. Development of technology centers and promotion of information literacy.

Many factors are responsible for a change in the landscape of libraries; a single factor cannot change the situation entirely. Libraries have changed from time to time and they have to change in the future too. Some of the important factors that helped the libraries to change are information explosion, growth in publications, customers' expectations, rising expenditure and shrinking resources, rise of competitors, information technologies and digital based resources. The past two decades have seen a great deal of change due to IT resulting in a demand for new patterns of scholarly information. These technological advancements have made significant impact on the growth of knowledge and unlocking of human potential. In library environment, the impact is clearly visible on information resources, services, and people. Some of the notable impacts have been given below.

COMPONENTS OF INFORMATION TECHNOLOGY

In 1960s the IBM invented computers for computing scientific calculations. Sun Micro Systems (2003) the automation process started its journey in 1970s with the introduction computing machines in libraries for scientific calculations. The next phase was development of integrated library systems (ILS) to perform library functions online and ILS led the emergence of MARC. Networking became a focus during 1980s and network supported ILS software developed during this period. This trend required re-education of the library staff, significant cost, more powerful technologies' software and networking configurations that were no longer developed in-house. Libraries began utilizing new application systems for automation of resource sharing, union catalogues and inter-library loan modules.

As the 1980s ended, libraries and computing centres were tackling communications, relational databases, and information distribution challenges. It became key factor for universities to provide their campuses with communication technologies that wired libraries and classrooms. Intranets provided campus connectivity using TCP/IP communication standards.

This permitted interconnectivity of computing resources: servers, PC desktops, and terminals. With the Internet becoming as defining technology, the 1990s saw greater use of campus communication infrastructures and commercial communication systems to create and store information and then to deliver it from libraries to end users. Large databases from periodical, magazine and journal publishers became increasingly available in digital format-at first on CD-ROM; later via online services. Library services are transitioning from local traditional collections to global resources provided on demand via the most advanced networking technologies. Today, library collections are used by people on campus as well as by individuals who are not even located on the library's physical facilities. Thus, individuals associated with a given institution and accessing resources from afar need new electronic interface tools. As a result, professional librarians must be computer literate and knowledgeable about Internet technologies to fully participate in the planning, design, and implementation of future library services.

During the period 1998-2002 the Internet, the web, computer languages and tools have matured to enable creation of rapidly increasing number of digital resources that need to be controlled, served and preserved by libraries.

Open archives initiative (OAI), metadata, Unicode etc. are the trends during that period. In the recent years the management of digital resources is occupying the prominent place. With resources growing at an exponential rate the ability of patrons to find what they want is more difficult. So, a well arranged collection of e-resources is very essential.

Information technology is a broad term that encompasses wide range of sub technologies. It is the convergence of computers, communication and microelectronic based technologies. Successive developments in information technology are tremendously enhancing their capabilities resulting into better technological devices, innovations, products, services and quality solutions.

Computer

A computer is an electronic device that manipulates information, or "data." It has the ability to store, retrieve, and process data. In 1943 development begins on the Electronic Numerical Integrator and Computer (ENIAC) in earnest at Penn State, Designed by John Mauchly and J. Presper Eckert of Moore School. In 1944, the Havard Mark I is introduced. Based on a series of proposals from Howard Aiken in the late 1930's, the Mark I compute complex tables for the U.S. Navy. It uses a paper tape to store instructions and Aiken hires Grace Hopper ("Amazing Grace") as one of three programmers working on the machine. Thomas J. Watson Sr. plays a pivotal role involving his company, IBM, in the machine's development. Work completes on ENIAC in 1946. Although only three years old the machine is woefully behind on technology, but the inventors opt to continue while working on a more modern machine, the EDVAC. Programming ENIAC requires it to be rewired. A later version eliminates this problem. To make the machine appear more impressive to reporters during its unveiling, a team member (possibly Eckert) puts translucent spheres (halved ping pong balls) over the lights. The US patent office will later recognize this as the first computer.

IBM introduces the 701 the following year. It is the first commercially successful computer. In 1956 FORTRAN is introduced. Two additional languages, LISP and COBOL, are added in 1957 and 1958. Other early languages include ALGOL and BASIC. Although never widely used, ALGOL is the basis for many of today's languages.

In 1961 Fairchild Semiconductor introduces the integrated circuit. Within ten years all computers use these instead of the transistor. Formally building sized computers are now room-sized, and are considerably more powerful. It becomes operational, displaying many of the features that make today's systems so powerful including virtual memory, pipeline instruction execution and paging.

On April 7, 1964, IBM introduces the System 360. While a technical marvel, the main feature of this machine is business oriented. IBM guarantees the "upward compatibility" of the system, reducing the risk that a business would invest in outdated technology. Dartmouth College, where the first network was demonstrated 25 years earlier, moves to the forefront of the "computer age" with the introduction of TSS (Time Share System) a crude(by today's standards) networking system. It is the first Wide Area Network. In 1975 the first personal computer is marketed in kit form. The Altair features 256 bytes of memory. Bill Gates, with others, writes a BASIC compiler for the machine. The next year Apple begins to market PC's, also in kit form. It includes a monitor and keyboard. During the next few years the personal computer explodes on the American scene i.e Microsoft, Apple and many smaller PC related companies form. By 1977 stores begin to sell PC's. Continuing today, companies strive to reduce the size and price of PC's while increasing capacity. Entering the fray, IBM introduces its PC in 1981. Time selects the computer as its Man of the Year in 1982. Tron, a computer-generated special effects extravaganza is released the same year (Leon, 1998).

Microcomputers : Microcomputers are the most common type of computers used by people today, whether in a workplace, at school or on the desk at home. The term "microcomputer" was introduced with the advent of single chip microprocessors. The term "microcomputer" itself is now practically an anachronism.

Minicomputers : A minicomputer is a class of multi-user computers that lies in the middle range of the computing spectrum, in between the smallest multi-user systems (mainframe computers) and the largest single-user systems (microcomputers or personal computers). The contemporary term for this class of system is midrange computer, such as the higher-end SPARC, POWER and Itanium based systems from Sun Microsystems, IBM and Hewlett-Packard.

Mainframe computers : The term mainframe computer was created to distinguish the traditional, large, institutional computer intended to service multiple users from the smaller, single user machines. These computers are capable of handling and processing very large amounts of data quickly. Mainframe computers are used in large institutions such as government, banks and large corporations.

Supercomputer : A supercomputer is focused on performing tasks involving intense numerical calculations such as weather forecasting, fluid dynamics, nuclear simulations, theoretical astrophysics, and complex scientific computations. A supercomputer is a computer that is at the frontline of current processing capacity, particularly speed of calculation. The term supercomputer itself is rather fluid, and the speed of today's supercomputers tends to become typical of tomorrow's ordinary computer. Supercomputer processing speeds are measured in floating point operations per second or FLOPS. An example of a floating point operation is the calculation of mathematical equations in real numbers. In terms of computational capability, memory size and speed, I/O technology, and topological issues such as bandwidth and latency, supercomputers are the most powerful, are very expensive, and not cost-effective just to perform batch or transaction processing. Transaction processing is handled by less powerful computers such as server computers or mainframes.

1. Hardware

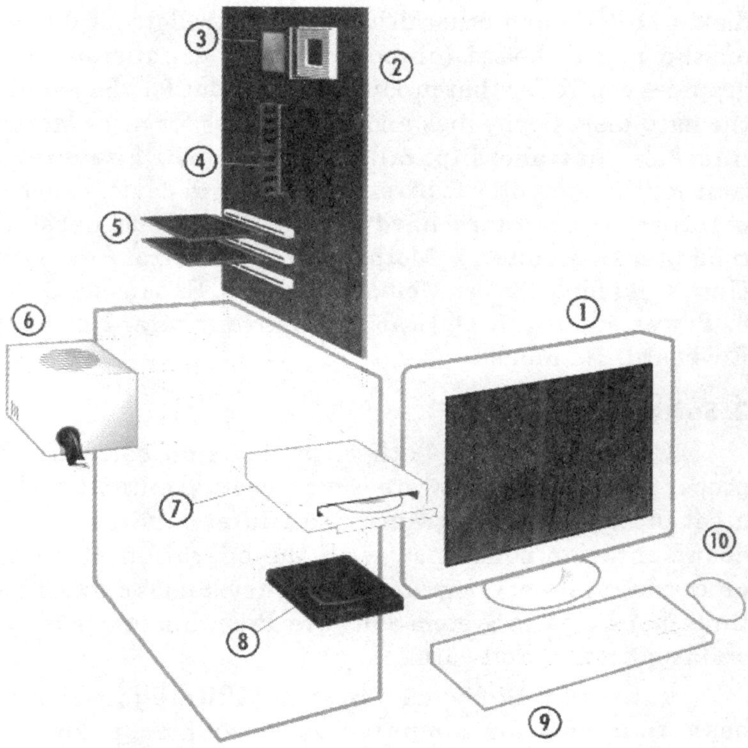

Hardware is a comprehensive term for all of the physical parts of a computer, as distinguished from the data it contains or operates on, and the software that provides instructions for the hardware to accomplish tasks. The boundary between hardware and software is slightly blurry - firmware is software that is "built-in" to the hardware, but such firmware is usually the province of computer programmers and computer engineers in any case and not an issue that computer users need to concern themselves with. A typical computer (Personal Computer, PC) contains in a desktop or tower case the following parts: Motherboard which holds the CPU, main memory and other parts, and has slots for expansion cards power supply - a case that holds a transformer, voltage control and fan storage controllers, of IDE, SCSI or other type, that control hard disk , floppy disk, CD-ROM and other drives; the controllers sit directly on the motherboard (on-board) or on expansion cards graphics controller that produces the output for the monitor the hard disk, floppy disk and other drives for mass storage interface controllers (parallel, serial, USB, Firewire) to connect the computer to external peripheral devices such as printers or scanners hardware of a modern personal computer: 1. Monitor, 2. Motherboard, 3. Central Processing Unit, 4. Random Access Memory (RAM), 5. Expansion Cards, 6. Power supply, 7. Optical Disc Drive, 8. Hard drive, 9. Keyboard, 10. Mouse.

2. Software

Computer needs both hardware and software for proper functioning. Software is a conceptual entity which is a set of computer programs, procedures, and associated documentation concerned with the operation of a data processing system. Computer software system is divided into three major classes System Software, Programming Software and Application Software.

1. System Software : System software provides the basic functions for computer usage and helps run the computer hardware and system. It includes a combination of the device drivers, operating systems, servers, utilities, window systems. System software is responsible for managing a variety of independent hardware components, so that they can work together harmoniously. Its purpose is to unburden the application software programmer from the often complex details of the particular computer being used, including such accessories as communications devices, printers, device readers, displays and keyboards, and also to partition the computer's resources such as memory and processor time in a safe and stable manner.

2. Programming Software : Programming software usually provides tools to assist a programmer in writing computer programs, and software using different programming languages in a more convenient way. The tools include compilers, debuggers, interpreters, linkers, text editors. An Integrated Development Environment (IDE) is a single application that attempts to manage all these functions.

3. Application Software : Application software is developed to aid in any task that benefit from computation. It is a broad category, and encompasses software of many kinds, including the internet browser being used to display this page. This category includes business software, computer-aided design, databases, decision making software, educational software, image editing, industrial automation, mathematical software etc.

4. Artificial Intelligence (AI) : It is the science and engineering of making intelligent machines, especially intelligent computer programs. It is related to the similar task of using computers to understand human intelligence. Artificial Intelligence is a combination of computer science, physiology, and philosophy. It is a broad topic, consisting of different fields, from machine vision to expert systems. The element that the fields of Artificial Intelligence have in common is the creation of machines that can "think". Artificial Intelligence refers to computer programmes, which emulate human intelligence. Examples are making decisions, solving problems and drawing conclusions. Artificial Intelligence techniques are being increasingly utilized to enhance database systems especially their user-friendliness. It has two branches: natural language processing and expert systems.

5. Natural Language Processing : In natural language processing, a user can interact with a computing system using everyday language rather than a structured command language with the help of an interface called natural language interface, which translates the natural language into the application language.

6. Expert System : An expert system can solve real-world problems using human knowledge and following human reasoning skills. Knowledge and thinking processes of experts are collected and encoded into a knowledge base. From that point on, the expert system could replace or assist the human experts in making complex decisions by integrating all the knowledge it has in its knowledge base. An expert system can be defined as Artificial Intelligence programmes designed to represent human expertise in a specific domain. The heart of an expert system is knowledge base, which contains facts, rules and other information pertaining to a particular domain. Facts represent accepted knowledge in a certain field (normally possessed by experts) and rules- a collection of F - THEN statements also called "rules of thumb" for drawing inferences. If such-and-such is true THEN assume that so and so is true. Typical expert system application areas include medical diagnosis, planning, decision-making, monitoring and design.

7. Databases : A database is an organized collection of data for one or more purposes, usually in digital form. The data are typically organized to model relevant aspects of reality, in a way that supports processes requiring this information. The term "database" refers both to the way its users view it, and to the logical and physical materialization of its data, content, in files, computer memory, and computer data storage. This definition is very general, and is independent of the technology used. However, not every collection of data is a database; the term database implies that the data is managed to some level of quality (measured in terms of accuracy, availability, usability, and resilience) and this in turn often implies the use of a general-purpose Database management system (DBMS). A general-purpose DBMS is typically a complex software system that meets many usage requirements, and the databases that it maintains are often large and complex. The utilization of databases is widely spread to a degree that virtually any technology and product nowadays rely on databases and DBMS for their development and commercialization, or even may have such embedded in them. Also organizations and companies, from small to very large, heavily depend on databases for their operations. The term database is correctly applied to the data and their containing data structures, and not to the DBMS which is a software system used to manage the data. The structure of a database is generally too complex to be handled without its DBMS, and any attempt to do otherwise is very likely to result in database corruption. DBMS are packaged as computer software products: well-known and highly utilized products include the Oracle DBMS, Access and SQL Server from Microsoft, DB2 from IBM and the Open source DBMS MySQL. Each such DBMS product currently supports many thousands of databases all over the world. The stored data in a database is not generally portable across different DBMS, but different DBMS can inter-operate to some degree (while each DBMS type controls a database of its own database type) to support together a single application using standards like SQL and ODBC. A successful general-purpose DBMS is designed in such a way that it can satisfy as many different applications and application designers and builders as possible. A DBMS also needs to provide effective run-time execution to properly support as many end-users as needed. Sometimes the combination of a database and its respective DBMS is referred to as a Database system (DBS).

TRENDS OF TECHNOLOGY

One of the undeniable facts associated with computer and communications technologies is that emerging technologies are being adopted with increasing speed by the market place. Thus librarians need to be aware of some of the more significant technologies trends likely to impact libraries in the future. These technologies challenges to libraries to address issues such as service delivery add value for its patrons and support new ways to deliver information to the library customer wherever that customer is located.

As current emerging technologies are adopted some other are replaced by even newer emerging technologies. Thus technology trends will be constantly evolving and changing over time. The Internet has impact libraries directly as more students and other individuals visit Web sites to find bibliographic citations and full text of journal articles to complete projects and other homework assignments, rather than visiting a library. Thus the libraries should aware of the new technology trends such as:

1. Telecommunication and Networking

Rapid advances in communication technology combined with accelerating developments in computer technology have offered tremendous opportunities in the field of information management, developments in communication technology have made possible to access a wide variety of electronic information resources across the globe easily, instantaneously and economically. Computers are used for generation, processing and storage of information. To make the information more useful and easily accessible remotely, it must be transferred from one location to another. The technology used in transferring information is called communication technology. Communication Technology consists of telecommunications and data communications. Telecommunications is the use of telephone, fax, telegraph, radio or television facilities to transfer the information, either directly or via computer. Data communication is the transfer of data or information between computers. It is the transmission or reception of digital information between two or more computers. Communication system consists of a transmitter, a channel and a receiver. It transmits information from transmitter to receiver through a channel. According to Rowley (1993), the essential components of a communication are a transmitter to send information, and receiver to accept it; a transmission medium (channel) through which the message travels; signals and codes which represent message; and network controls to ensure that the message gets to its destination.

The physical components of communication technology include cabling media. Switching and signaling technologies, communication controls, protocols, codes and standards, digital or analog communications and data or voice communication technologies. The important applications of communication technologies in information services include access to databases and digital information resources by remote users electronic file transfer, electronic messaging, electronic data interchange and sending online databases as well as network databases etc.

2. TCP/ IP

The number of people connecting to the Internet will continue to grow for the foreseeable future. With increasing frequency computer chips are being installed in a wide variety of devices ranging from automobiles to vending machines to clothing and these devices are being connected to the Internet. TCP/IP provides telephone services via the Internet (called telephony) desktop video conferencing, audio and video broadcasting and soon on-demand movies. The reason for all of this activity is that using TCP/IP Significantly decreases the complexity and. therefore, the cost of providing the service.

Today because everybody is linked, more goods and services gain their value from this widespread Network Effect. One of the implications of making connections to all of these devices is that a wide range of services is now available without regard to distance. No longer is it necessary to visit a bank branch, be physically present to attend a university call a broker to execute a stock transaction, or obtain a cost quote for insurance, a product or a service. All of this and much more is now being accomplished using the Internet. Consequently a library must consider and identify ways that it can provide some or all of its services without requiring the customer to physically visit the library. Whether it is document delivery online 24/7 reference services borrowing of materials. Or providing access to online databases libraries must change the way they provide services.

3. Peer-To-Peer Networking

The fundamental idea behind peer-to-peer (P2P) networking is simplicity itself: you share files, programs, and computer processing cycles, and communicate directly with other people over the Internet without having to rely on a centralized server; the end result is the prospect of distributed file systems, distributed search engines, virtual super computers, and so much more. This idea has been applied in several interesting ways, ranging from sharing music files using collaborative software with a shared workspace, sharing "idle" computer processing cycles, and so forth. If you have used instant messaging, then you have used a P2P program. The whole idea ofP2P software is to eliminate the middleman (the server on the network).

i. P2P computing differs from client/server in three fundamental ways:

ii. In P2P processing, the exchange of services is symmetric (I.e., it is happening between peers running identical software and having roughly the same processing power) and each computer has equivalent responsibility.

iii. In client/server, there is a one-to-many relationship-one server supports many clients. In P2P processing, there are many cooperating peers, and any of them can initiate an interaction or transaction with another peer.

iv. The client/server interaction has a fixed capacity, while P2P provides transparent access to services of any kind with an almost unlimited capacity.

v. P2P collaborative software allows groups to share information and documents among themselves, across an entire organization, or with outside groups. This approach has the potential for significantly improving the productivity among all employees within an organization. Such scftware allows people to route documents, electronically annotate each other's work, view ideas on a white board, have online discussions, and so forth. Any work done offline is immediately shared and updated as soon as you connect to the network. P2P computing offers the opportunity to reduce centralized computer resources and eliminate redundant computer storage. P2P search engines offer the prospect of using metadata (e.g. the XML-based Dublin Core) to describe and classify information found at a Web site. The Dublin Core combined with the RDF a data model and XML serialization syntax for describing resources means that new approaches can be used to overcome the serious limitations of the existing Web search engines.

4. XML

XML is a simpler version of the original and more complex SGML but designed specifically for the Web. Using the XML organizations can define, transmit, validate and interpret data between applications and databases. XML provides structure rather than being a presentation system. XML separates the underlying data from how the data is displayed; thus the data itself can be more easily organized, programmed, edited, and exchanged between Web sites and applications. XML and its associated DTD play an important role in the exchange of information.

5. Voice and Translation Capabilities

Speech recognition is actually a combination of computer hardware and software that recognizes spoken words. However, major improvements have been made in continuous speech systems-voice recognition systems that allow the individual to speak naturally and usually do not require users to teach the system how to recognize their voice. Such systems are useful in instances when the user is unable to use a keyboard to enter data or the individual has a low typing speed. Voice-based browser technology is promising full-fledged access tc Internet services from any telephone. Voice XML2.0 a draft standard being worked on by W3C, is a standard markup language for voice data and it will provide a common means for integrating touch pad signals synthesized speech and speech recognition within a Web-based application. Voice XML is a server-driven technology. One of the by-products of computer-telephony integration is that TCP/IP will be used to place phone calls or deliver a fax. There already are Web sites that will translate a Web page from one language to another.

6. Web Services

Web services are applications that have been enabled to use a standard universal language to send data and instructions to one another, with no data translation or conversion required. Because the internet is being used the connection problems are minimized or eliminated. To date, most data and information that is accessible via the Internet is viewed by people using a browser; thus the Internet can be thought of as "people-centric." To be used by an application within an organization the information must either be "scraped" from the screen or sent by the information supplier. Web services are likely to be at the heart of the next generation of distributed services.

7. Internet

Internet is one of the most important landmark developments in the field of information technology. Internet is the world's largest and fastest growing network of networks. Internet is growing at an astounding rate connecting millions of users located all over the world. The user's figures vary widely and change very rapidly day by day. Internet contains wealth of information resources on almost all the fields of knowledge. Internet is the world's largest computer network, the network of networks, scattered the entire world. "Internet" is a group of two or more networks that are:

i. It interconnected physically capable of communicating and sharing data with each other able to act together as a single network.

ii. Machines on one network can communicate with machines on other networks, and data, files, and other information back and forth. For this to work, the networks and machines that are part of the Internet have to either to speak the same "language" when they are communicating or to use an "interpreter". This "language" is software that enables the different types of machines on separate networks to communicate and exchange information. The Internet, with a capital "I," is the network of networks, which either uses the TCP/ IP protocol or interacts with TCP/ IP network via gateways. The Internet covers the globe and includes large, international networks as well as many smaller, local area networks (LANs). The Internet offers access to data, graphics, sound, software, text, and people through a variety of services and tools for communication and data exchange.

iii. Internet provides various search engines tools to facilitate easy searching and location of specific required information. The important search engines include Alta Vista, Excite, Google, HotBot, Infoseek, Lycos, Gopher, Yahoo, Web crawler. Magellan etc. Internet offers a wide range of services which include electronic mail, bulletin board service, discussion forums, network newsgroups, electronic conferences, electronic commerce, electronic marketing etc.

Internet is a way in which various applications and services are linked-and almost every library and organization is linked to the Internet.

Interoperability : Any Web service can interact with any other Web service. Web services can run on any platform and can be written in any programming language.

Low barrier to entry : The concepts behind Web

services are easy to understand. They offer a more flexible or loosely coupled way of linking applications. In addition, free toolkits are being provided by a host of vendors that allow developers to more quickly develop and deploy Web services. Web services are a way to link existing applications rather than a platform for new development.

Ubiquity : Because Web services rely on HTTP and XML any device that supports these technologies can both host and access Web services. Even wireless services can be provided using Web services.

Industry support : All major vendors support and are involved with extending the standards around which Web services are built.

8. Social Networking (Web 2.0) and Blogs

Today, the terms like Web 2. 0 and blogging are the buzzwords. Along with web 2.0, blogging is also getting popularity among the library professionals. Weblog or blog is the website consisting of journal like entries that are arranged in reverse chronologically order. These are distinguished by their frequent, usually short, post, and by the way they reflect their owner's personality. Weblogs or the blogs are the sites that capture particular views, ideas, or opinions overtime. These are the web applications, which contain periodic posts on a common web page. These posts are often but not necessarily in reverse chronological order. Each blog tells a story, be it about a person, an organization, an event, or any other subject such as the environment, healthcare, disasters, language, literature, etc. The person who maintains a blog is called a blogger and the act of creating and maintaining a blog is called blogging. In a blog, the entries are read, commented on, and discussed by an even larger community, often fostering active debate. This may sound similar to a listserv and, in some ways, it is. However, unlike a listserv, blogs are typically accessible to the public at large, thereby encouraging more diverse readership and disseminating information further and with greater speed. The hyper textual, link-centric nature of weblog entries further facilitates this rapid exchange and distribution of information.

A number of Internet search engines and directories such Yahoo and Google, provide information about blog and lists of weblogs, and some include page from weblogs in their search results. In addition, weblog creation site such as Blogger maintain lists of weblogs that have been created using their services. Ramos and Piper (2006) state that there are now some specialist weblog search engines, the largest of which are Google (http://blogsearch.google.com) and Technorati. (http://www.technorati.com). The same criteria that you use to evaluate a website for accuracy, currency, and authority should also apply to blogs. It is speculated that a primary use for blogs in reference would be for the most cutting-edge material, things that have not yet made it into the regular literature channels.

Blogs are perfect for dissemination of information as the system of dated entries makes it easy for viewers to identify new content. A number of the system's libraries have caught the fever as well. The growth of library weblogs has noticeable growth during last several years. As such, libraries must follow new technologies very closely and the advantages of the newest innovations, such as Blogs and RSS feeds and these must be reflected in library services. Despite the increasing popularity of blogs, few libraries have taken advantage of what they offer.

9. Wireless Connections/ Mobile Communications

In the era of improved mobile communication technologies, vast amount of changes are generated in facilitating communication and the transfer of information namely from business to business, business to customers, employers to employees, etc. and in providing more and more added value services (Steenderen, 2002). The technologies have made communication and access to information very convenient and timely to the users from the comfort of their own home and office, and from where ever they are while on the move with their mobile phone units or PDAs. The use of mobile technologies is increasingly widespread. Various applications can be observed among the users, which ranged from telephone conversation and simple text messages (SMS), to multimedia messaging services (MMS) and internet access, depending on the capability of each mobile phone technology and services rendered. These applications have been made possible through various developments in the mobile telephone technology such as GPRS, WAP, and the 3G standard. Mayer (2002) has introduced several steps through which institutions may follow in providing SMS services. The steps involved collection of mobile phone numbers, setting up a centralized SMS service centre, and sending group SMS via a network. According to him, the information that can be applied in a centralized SMS is, such as "Reading lists the list of the books, which are in the library; lectures, meeting schedule, exam dates; academic information about the students; crucial homework reminders; web link; urgent messaging; announcements thought/facts of the week, information about new activities, changes in schedules; and Mobile author application: it will help lecturers / teachers/ instructors/ tutors to create and author their computer-based courses".

Wireless technology has the potential to offer many new possibilities for accessing information from online catalogues, online databases, the internet and virtual libraries. Among the wireless technologies includes digital cellular technologies, packet radio and wireless local area networks.

10. Digitization

The applications of digital technologies within libraries began with the development of turnkey software solutions. In the 1990s libraries extended their collections by promoting access to licensed databases, often connecting end users to these resources via the Internet using a Web-based interface.

The next logical step being taken by many libraries is to augment their physical collections and licensed resources with links to special collections selected from among the growing base of digital library development projects. The Web-based interfaces developed by specific library institutions connect all these resources in a potentially seamless fashion. This is the role of practical digital library development to augment the collections of existing libraries and to extend the range of resources available to end users.

Technology remains one of the primary drivers of change in the ways that people work, seek information, communicate, and entertain themselves. In an academic environment, no unit has been transformed by technology than library. The libraries need to reorganize their physical space to make technology-enabled resources both more readily available and widely used. The penetration of technology in libraries is more visible since the invention of computers. Information Technology (IT) has been undergoing rapid revolutionary developments for the last four decades due to its most distinguishing features of decreasing cost, size and increasing capabilities and pervasiveness.

2

Information Technology in Libraries

Rapid advances in Information Technology in the past two decades have brought revolutionary changes in the concept, organization, functioning and management of library and information systems throughout the world. Information technologies today are characterized by their very dynamic development and increasing complexity. Information Technology not only affects the technical services of libraries but also shapes the library services that are being offered to the public. Information technology application in library and information field has made remarkable progress in the world.

Information technology is the collective term for various technologies involved in processing and transmitting information that may include computing, telecommunications and microelectronics. The IT enables society to work expeditiously and also provides decision makers with the opportunity to consider more data in decision-making. Hence the definition of information has broadened due to the role of non-print material that is stored electronically. A good example in this direction is the World Wide Web, that covers a vast repository of information or data, which may be accessed from any part of the globe and at any point in time.

INFORMATION TECHNOLOGY AND LIBRARIES

The extent to which technology has come to dominate the library management debate is not surprising. The challenges posed by current and emerging technologies cannot be overemphasized and the frequent use of the term "revolution" to characterize the present situation seems appropriate. Even after thirty years of computerization, most of us remain incapable of grasping the magnitude and long-term implications of the changes that are taking place. The growth of the Internet and its popularization across the globe, along with the immense potential of emerging high-speed, satellite-based communication technologies, provide ample justification for our desire to search for terms that capture the essence of what we are experiencing and what may lie ahead. Our daily lives personal and professional already reflect the convergence of digital information technologies with the human experience. From homes to schools to hospitals to small businesses to high-tech agencies to libraries, digital information technologies are drastically transforming the cultural, social, psychological, and economic landscape. This is true not only in developed nations but also in those that are sometimes characterised as "third world nations".

LIBRARIANSHIP AND TECHNOLOGY

As a first step in the development of an understanding of the times we live in and the challenges faced by our profession, we need to recognize that although the definition of librarianship does not include a semantic dimension of "technology", the practice of librarianship constitutes technological practice. This may not make intuitive sense at first, since we always associate the concept of technology with physical artifacts. However, librarianship comprises knowledge, a belief system, as well as tools and machines. From a conceptual standpoint and following Franklin's model, librarianship is also the collection of procedures we use to accomplish our professional mission. Librarianship is about accepted conventions and routines. The adoption of a certain way of doing what we do is what gives us a professional identity and is what separates the outsiders from the insiders. Leaving aside the question of the requirements that need to be fulfilled for an occupation to be rewarded with the highly desirable label of "profession", librarianship is about practice and the way in which we integrate knowledge and artifacts to accomplish something. Librarianship is not changing as a result of the introduction of computing or networking technologies. From a historical standpoint, libraries have always relied on the use of the latest technologies to fulfill their function; paper, typewriters, microfiche or microfilm readers, etc. Librarians have always relied on the use of tools to fulfill the needs of the communities they serve. In libraries, for instance, typewriters were once used to prepare book order and to facilitate the production of cataloging records. However, technologies are not always just about facilitating the execution of work-related tasks. They are also about control. The use of computers and software designed to support the creation of cataloging records, for instance, is not only about efficiency. Cataloging support systems can be used to link the work of catalogers, control productivity, and create an environment of control (Sierpe, 2004).

The transformations relate to a shift in the values that underlie professional, that is, technological practice. From being primarily centered and focused on supporting learning communities, that is, being user- or human-centered, the profession is changing course and becoming information- or technology-centered. These changes are not related to technology per-se or the introduction of the latest computing systems. What the changes suggest is that the profession has changed its direction and realigned its values with the demands of an age where efficiency, productivity, corporate interests, and profits, are highlighted while the social and human costs are ignored.

APPLICATION OF INFORMATION TECHNOLOGY (IT) IN LIBRARIES

Worldwide libraries have been exploring new technologies for providing better and faster access to vast information resources and efficient information services to their users. Information Technology has offered better solutions to achieve greater level of efficiency, productivity and excellence services in libraries. Information Technology is also fulfills the 4th law of Dr. S. R. Ranganathan "Save the time of Reader. The application and accessibility of information technology facilitates the free flow of information, creative expression and effective management. The major factors and challenges forced the libraries to adopt Information Technology such as: information explosion, technological development, provide efficient and effective services, increased the number of users, increased the expectations of the users, online information retrieval, increase the commercial information providers, changes the nature of Information resources (E-Journals, CD-ROMs, and Online Databases, etc.) .

Kumar (1993) presented a report about the application of modern technologies in health science libraries in India and tackled issues on the usage of technologies such as photocopying, microfilming, computers, facsimile transmission, audiovisual media, online searching and CD-ROM. Mujoo-Munish and Virmalhan (1998) in their paper 'Information Technology Concerns and Issues in Developing Countries' gave the practical example of India, focusing on the strengths of India's knowledge base that were to be applied in order to overcome her weaknesses. Chopra and Mukherjee (2000) traced the need for networking among academic libraries by pointing out the basic targets and also discussed the need for and usefulness of local area networking within the university and other academic institutions. Rao (2001) reported the paradigm changes that libraries undergo and the challenges to their networking, and also highlighted the role of information technology in transforming traditional library services into digital mode. Singh (2001) described the state of computerization among the six institutes of information technology. Kannappanavar and Vijayakumar (2001) shed light on the use of hardware and software in University of Agricultural Science libraries in Karnataka and also highlighted access to networks, information services and barriers in information technology (IT) applications.

Library Automation is one of the major applications of information technology in libraries. It is helped to change the library In-house activities (Acquisition, Cataloguing, Indexing, Serial control, Circulation etc.) from manual system to automation. In 1980s, most of the libraries were computerized their in-house activities in world. Recently, libraries have to implement increasingly complex solutions that involve distributed networking and access to remote information resources. The use of information technology in libraries has tremendously increased due to its enhanced user satisfaction, cost effectiveness, faster and simpler programs, rapid communicative interaction and easier operational procedures. The library and information centres are increasingly being called upon to provide more relevant, up-to-date and timely information to a wide range of users. To satisfy the varied needs, they require availability and accessibility to a variety of information resources. The electronic resources that are available in libraries today are an outcome of the advances in both computer technologies, including information storage and delivery mechanisms (such as CDROMs), and software providing user-friendly interfaces. In most of the academic libraries in the Western countries, Online Public Access Catalogues (OPACs) have almost replaced card catalogues, offering enhanced search capabilities for accessing the local collection; they often include the holdings of other area or regional libraries, as well. Many libraries also provide a web interface to their library and information system, often including direct links to electronic journals, books and Internet resources.

University libraries have made substantial progress in the implementation of information technology applications in the library.

INFORMATION TECHNOLOGY FEATURES IN LIBRARIES

Libraries are coming to terms with the new economic and technological realities that began back in the 1980s. Many libraries in the developed countries have already shifted gear and those in developing countries are slowly replacing their cumbersome manual procedures with more effective computer and telecommunications systems. Further, they are developing efficient resource-sharing capabilities by participating in networks. It should be observed that where the technology is in place the institutions have totally changed. The following are taken to be part of Information Technology (Kemparaju and Nyamboga. 2001):

1. automation (online public catalogue, cataloguing, acquisition, periodicals control, circulation and reference)
2. electronic mail, electronic bulletin boards and electronic conferencing
3. telecommunications (networks)
4. Compact Disc-Read Only Memory (CD-ROM)
5. telefacsimile (fax)
6. personal computer applications
7. Reprographic technologies (photocopy, microfilm, optical/digital and audio/video).

LIBRARY AUTOMATION

Technology has shifted the patron's expectations, changing the library's role from a collection of materials to an information provider and mediator. Computers are used in libraries to perform clerical duties; to produce a wide variety of products, such as bibliographic lists and all sorts of statistical reports, including catalog records; and to help in many activities, such as circulation. Furthermore, computers are used to promote the sharing of catalog records worldwide, saving time and effort for countless libraries.

An automated library is an online catalog in which all of the library's collection is stored in a database and available on a computer. Library users can not only find materials in the library by searching the author, title, or subject, but also may use many new features as they are made available in the automated environment. This includes more searching strategies, such as keyword and Boolean searching, linking of other databases to offer more materials and information, and linking the online database to automated circulation, cataloging, and acquisitions systems. Furthermore, the online catalog has the capacity of providing full text indexing. Electronic books and journals can also display in full text on the online catalog.

Mostly libraries approach the automation issue in two ways: using the integrated system or the single-function system. The integrated system is a complete system composed of all library functions using the same database. Typically, it includes a circulation module, a cataloging module, an acquisitions module, and a serials module. Integrated library systems encompass a variety of library operations. By sharing the same database, one computer system can serve several modules for applications in cataloging, acquisition, serials control, circulation, and the online public access catalog. The system also allows the online public access catalog to link to the commercially available online reference services such as abstracting, indexing, and full-text reference databases. The library purchases from the vendor not only the system but a package that includes hardware, installation, staff training, subsequent software upgrades, troubleshooting help, and system consultation.

AUTOMATION OF TECHNICAL SERVICES

Although all library functions have been affected by

the use of computers, the technical services area has changed most. Traditional card preparation has become database management. Earlier Catalogers were spent hours doing original cataloging or searching in bibliographic listing. Now days developed the machine readable catalogue. Cataloging has become a quick process in which a record is downloaded for local use without much alteration. This development has helped to reduce the costs of cataloging, cataloging staff has switched from librarians to library technicians, and, because one record is utilized by thousands of libraries, uniformity has resulted as strict standards are adhered to. All clerical functions are eliminated. The need for knowledgeable manipulation and maintenance of these databases has significantly increased the visibility of technical services, as the cataloging done behind the scenes becomes instantly accessible in the public catalog ton thousands of library users.

Automation has changed the acquisitions function from being repetitive and tedious to being a quick, efficient process. The goal of automation in technical services is to increase productivity, to eliminate duplicated effort in organizing materials, to increase the efficiency of operation, and, eventually, to enhance library services.

In an automated technical services operation, productivity will be increased. With the same number of staff, more tasks can be accomplished, and they can be done better. The information must be input once, then the computer takes care of the tedious jobs of indexing and filing, saving staff time to work on more meaningful tasks. In an automated catalog, human mistakes are exposed instantly, allowing correction measures to be taken quickly, resulting in a more accurate database and enabling the library to maintain a more efficient and effective technical services organization.

Because of the collective use of the integrated automation system, libraries are able to share resources. For example, original cataloging, which used to be the emphasis of a library technical services operation, has been almost eliminated. Most library materials are now copy cataloged, meaning that the cataloging needs to be done only once, usually by the Library of Congress or other large university or research library. All other libraries can take the information and attach a local record to it, saving hundreds of libraries not only staff time for redundant work but also staff expertise.

The computer revolution has had an overwhelming impact on libraries. Automation has become a fact of life in the library technical services area. Most libraries now use computers for at least part of the technical services operation, be it accessing national or regional databases for cataloging, linking directly to vendors for acquisitions, or using the complete integrated automation system, all of which facilitate the work in both technical services and the public services areas.

BENEFITS OF INFORMATION TECHNOLOGY (IT) IN LIBRARIES

Information Technology will help the growth and development of libraries in different directions. Some of the benefits and advantages of information technology are improved productivity, reduce staff, reduce unit cost of operations, improve control of library collection, reduce error, improve speed and access, remote access to users, retrieval unlimited information from numerous sources, and development of online resource sharing.

RESOURCE SHARING & NETWORKING OF LIBRARIES

Advancements in technology, coupled with the ever-changing needs of users, are pushing computer networking to new heights, both in terms of capabilities and the importance of sharing resources efficiently. Pong (1990) stated that the Singapore Integrated Library Automation Service (SILAS) system has 30 institutions with online access to the database via 116 terminals. The main function of SILAS is to provide online shared cataloguing facilities to participating libraries, which can cut down drastically the costly and time-consuming process of creating bibliographic records from scratch. Thus duplication of effort in cataloguing is avoided. For the network as a whole, the estimated average cataloguing hit rate is over 60% for libraries with general science and technology collection, the hit rates go beyond 80%. The availability of participant" s holdings information in national union catalogue facilitates inter-library loans and helps libraries in rationalizing their acquisitions.

In India, Delhi Library Network (DELNET) was started at the India International Centre Library in January 1988 and was registered as a society in 1992. It was initially supported by the National Information System for Science and Technology (NISSAT), Department of Scientific and Industrial Research, Government of India. It was subsequently supported by the National Informatics Centre, Department of Information Technology, Ministry of Communications and Information Technology, Government of India and Ministry of Culture, Government of India. DELNET has been established with the prime objective of promoting resource sharing among the libraries through the development of a network of libraries. It aims to collect, store, and disseminate information besides offering computerised services to users, to coordinate efforts for suitable collection development and also to reduce unnecessary duplication wherever possible (DELNET, 2011).

LIBRARY CONSORTIA

The emergence of Internet, particularly the World Wide Web (WWW) as a new media of information delivery and the E-content environment have been driving the emergence and popularity of newer and more effective models of information access and resource sharing around the world. An increasing number of publishers are using the Internet as a global way to offer their publications to the international community of scientists and technologists. Technology is in a position today to provide more content to more users at a significantly lower cost per user. The post-Internet era is 'witnessing a significant jump in the access to and usage of information. The combination of these developments has resulted in development of "Consortia-based subscription" to journals everywhere in the world.

STRATEGIC PLANNING FOR IMPLEMENTATION OF INFORMATION TECHNOLOGY (IT) IN LIBRARIES

Information Technology (IT) is a driving force for change in libraries. Libraries are experiencing enormous changes due to application of new technologies. The magnitude and speed of technological change in recent years has been phenomenal which may likely to continue at much faster rate in the foreseeable future. The rapid technological change and transformation has tremendous impact on organization's decision makers, library operations, resources, services, staff and users. A very rapid rate of technological innovations has made it imperative to consider technology as the crucial factor influencing the functioning and management of modem library. Information technology is transforming libraries at a speed unimaginable just a few decades ago. The most pronounced difference between the digital/virtual library of today and the traditional library of yester year is the result of rapid pace of technological change taking place in libraries.

In today's dynamic environment of the rapidly changing nature of technology, strategic planning for managing new technology has become more crucial for harnessing its fuel potential and benefits. The strategies enable not only in selecting and implementing right technologies but also help in identifying appropriate automated operations and services that would best meet the users' needs and fulfill the mission of the library. Libraries must develop their capabilities and design innovative strategies to keep abreast of technological changes and to harness full potential of new technology. The strategy of libraries to continuously embrace technological change and to manage new technologies has become essential for survival, growth, development and success.

Modern technologies have brought dramatic changes in today's library management and users expectations. Application of IT solutions to library operations and information services is a very complex and challenging process. Libraries are facing variety of issues, problems, threats and challenges in the introduction, use and management of new technologies. Identifying the problems, understanding the issues and formulation of sound strategies are the keys to the successful management of technological change in libraries. Libraries intending to use IT applications should have strategic planning, innovative ideas and intelligent strategies for successful implementation and utilization of modem technologies.

FACTORS IN STRATEGIC PLANNING FOR INFORMATION TECHNOLOGY (IT)

Libraries use IT to increase the efficiency and effectiveness of their operations and services. Information Technology is highly dynamic, fast changing and become obsolete so quickly in such a short span that even before one technology is fully received, understood implemented and used, an improved version or a new technology is being developed. One cannot service tomorrow's users with yesterday's technology. Constant up gradations in technology have become essential for survival and success. In fact keeping up with new technologies is the biggest problem faced by the people around the world. Practically, it is becoming increasingly difficult for the libraries to keep pace with these rapid technological changes especially in developing countries where resources are scarce.

Managing new technologies has become an expensive, complex and challenging task requiring the formulation of strategic planning and sound strategies to achieve success. Strategic planning is a key to the successful management of technological change in libraries. Implementation of IT to library operations is a complex and continuous process. It requires imaginative, intelligent planning and huge investment of financial as well as human resources. Libraries intending to use IT have to plan systematically well in advance for successful implementation to derive maximum benefit and to minimize problems. Libraries should develop a sound technology plan to make use of the new technologies in an efficient and cost effective manner. A number of factors like organizations environment, management support, leadership, financial resources, staff competence, users' information needs and expectations need to be studied for designing sound strategies for the management of technological change in libraries.

i. Organisational Environment : The introduction and use of new technologies in libraries will become quite easier and successful only when organizational environment is conducive and supportive. Toe environment for change is the state of organization's preparedness for acceptance and introduction of change. An environment that supports technological change in an organization's library would be one in which change is seen as a normal process, and in which the organizations decision makers, library users and library staff are familiar with technological developments and their potential application in the library (Klobas, 1990).

ii. Management Support : Since library is a part of a wider parent organization, librarian alone cannot take decision of IT implementation in library. He has to depend on management for taking such decision. As IT needs heavy investment, the whole-hearted support of management is essential for its successful implementation in library. Top management need to be fully involved right from the beginning of the technology planning process to the decisions concerning IT implementation in library. They should be persuaded, educated and convinced about the potential benefits of IT in various library operations and services to get their support and cooperation. The decision makers in the parent organization need to be made aware of the new developments and opportunities presented by the new technologies, if they are to support the change proposal and implementation process. They should be well informed about the progress of new technological developments through regular management meetings and sending technology update news bulletins periodically.

The responsibility of getting management support however has to be taken by professional librarian who must demonstrate a commitment to modernization including the use of IT for real benefits to the users' continuity. The most effective way of obtaining management support is via user groups. Librarians in India need to take a more proactive approach in influencing decisions concerning resource allocation for the modernization of libraries (Haravu, 1995).

iii. Leadership : The success of IT implementation depends to a great extent on the availability of competent leader with in the library. Leader is a driving force for implementation of new technologies in library. Librarian must play the role of a leader who must be committed and shoulder full responsibility from the planning stage to the successful completion of IT implementation process. He has to plan, direct, control and guides the change management process. He must be able to convince decision makers and communicate with all levels of staff members, interact with users and work in a team environment. The leader must forecast the emerging future technologies and strive to implement and promote their effective use of library services.

iv. Financial Resources : Financial resources are one of the most important factors contributing for the successful implementation of new technologies in libraries. IT needs heavy investment for its implementation in the library. Cost involved in acquisition of hardware, software, databases and computerization, networking and their continued maintenance is very large that many organizations are not able to take decisions so easily to invest in IT. Further, it is difficult to anticipate all costs associated with fast changing nature of emerging dynamic technologies. At the time of allocation of funds, library is being given low priority as compared to other departments in most of the organizations. As a result, libraries are not getting adequate financial resources required for procuring modem information technologies. Due to fast changing nature of technologies, obsolescence in information technology is so high that it is becoming increasingly difficult for libraries to keep pace with these new technologies without adequate resources. Adequate funds are essential for implementation of new technologies. Funds must be provided annually to install new technology or to maintain existing technology and to update or replace obsolete technology on a regular basis. Financial resources need to be planned carefully taking into account both current and future requirements for managing technological change in libraries.

Management must be made aware of the need, usefulness of IT and motivated to allocate more funds for introducing or up gradation of modem technologies in library management. Today, funds are being provided for modernization and implementation of new technologies in libraries in India by many external bodies viz. UGC, AICTE, CSIR, ICAR, ICMR, ICSSR, NISSAT and Department of Science and Technology. These bodies provide funds for projects related to IT applications in libraries. Librarians must submit well-prepared project proposals clearly indicating the objectives, activities, funds required and time schedules for implementation of new technologies in their libraries.

v. Staff Competence : One of the most important factors for successful implementation of information technology is the level of competence of the staff (Hofmann, 1995). One of the major problems in effective use of information technology in libraries is the shortage of technically skilled and competent manpower. Without adequate knowledge, staff members working at computers have to spend a lot of time for learning, experimenting and using IT applications in real situations.

vi. Staff Involvement : Staff acceptance is another important factor contributing to the successful use of IT in libraries. 0 new technologies will be successfully implemented without the acceptance, full support and commitment of all levels of library staff. It is a human tendency to resist change. As some of library staff still lacks knowledge of IT, they are not convinced of the use of IT and so not willing to respond positively to the change of new technologies. There is also a psychological fear in the minds of the library staff that the use of IT in libraries may lead to retrenchment/unemployment. It should be made clear to the staff that IT is used to introduce new services and make improvements and not to reduce either the existing library services/employees. Further they must be convinced that the rapid spread of IT use will lead to a tremendous demand for skilled personnel. Therefore, they must be assured that no one is going to loose his job as a result of the introduction of IT in libraries. The success of use of IT in library depends on the extent to which supervisory and operational staffs are involved in its planning, design, analysis and implementation. The psychological barriers to change must be cleared in the initial stage involving all the staff in its implementation.

Library staff involvement must be multifunctional and multilevel in the technology planning process. Staff involvement in planning process will create interest, improve motivation and ultimately extend full support and cooperation for successful implementation of new technologies. A number of committees and sub committees involving key persons from all levels of library staff are to be constituted in planning, decision-making and implementation of new technologies in libraries. Library staff should be kept informed periodically about the plans, decisions, activities and progress of the IT implementation process in the library.

vii. Staff Training : The successful implementation of new technologies can be achieved duly by involving, training and bringing the entire library staff together in a team so that they are motivated to contribute greater levels of performance. Library staff should be provided adequate training to have thorough understanding and knowledge of the IT potentials on library and information products and services. The knowledge, skill and interest in various aspects of IT will need to be constantly upgraded among the library staff. Due to fast changing technological developments, continuous in-service training for working library staff is essential for not only to keep they well informed about the latest developments in their fields but also to learn new skills in the use of modem information technologies. The introduction of new and advanced technologies into the libraries immediately results in different skill requirements. Once the decision to adopt a new technology has been made, management must anticipate and determine, before implementation, the skills necessary to run the new installations efficiently and effectively.

Library staff needs to keep abreast of recent developments in technological innovations through a variety of means such as books and journals, professional meetings, and continuing education programs. They must be sent to automate libraries for personal observation and practical experience in handling different technologies. Management must anticipate the skill requirements of new technologies scheduled for implementation and develop operational plans to match existing staff skills through retraining and relocating measures with minimal disruption to operations and minimal adverse effects on the existing staff.

viii. User Education : The success of IT implementation in libraries depends greatly on the extent of user's acceptance and their satisfaction. User is the kingpin of the library. Users should be kept well informed about new technological developments so that they can understand, accept and make more effective use of IT based new services. Informed users can appreciate and may even encourage the library or its parent organization to adopt new technologies.

Active marketing approach is the key for user acceptance. Higher levels of user acceptance and utilization can be achieved by well-designed training programme, effective marketing strategy and improved accessibility to computerized services.

ix. Communication : Implementation of new technologies in libraries affects different groups of people in various ways. These groups will need to be informed of different aspects of the process and progress of different stages of IT implementation in library. Effective communication at all stages with all the groups viz. decision makers, library staff, users and the technology vendors is essential for successful management of technological change in library. There are a variety of communication methods that can be used for different groups for different purposes. They include regular staff meetings, periodical technology update news bulletins and training progarmmes.

x. Safety and Security : Another important factor that deserves careful attention is the security and safety of data. Fire extinguishers and other safety measures are to be provided. The security problems faced in most of the libraries are theft, physical damage, loss of files etc.; Computer viruses are one of the most serious problems affecting the development and use of databases in libraries. The effect of virus ranges from humorous to the catastrophe. Computer users, professionals, organizations and institutions have been seriously affected in terms of losing valuable data and program files by the viruses. As library databases are usually huge and contain valuable data, it is necessary to protect expensive resources and data from mishandling, deletion, unauthorized access and viruses. A well planned security policy and program is essential to protect valuable electronic information resources. Backup facilities for storage and protection of data in the case of corruption of files have to provide on a regular basis. Use of anti-virus programs and passwords are the acceptable means of providing security. The computer room should be secure and accessible only to authorized persons.

STRATEGIES FOR MANAGING TECHNOLOGICAL CHANGES IN LIBRARIES

Library developments brought by the new information technologies in the past two decades have clearly demonstrated that the application of IT solutions in library is no longer a matter of choice but is a matter of survival in the global digital information era. Successful achievement of library goals and satisfaction of users rising expec4ttions in times of fast-changing technological environment demands the development of sound strategies. The management must formulate innovative and intelligent strategies which will contribute significantly to the successful management of technological change in libraries. The following are some of the important strategies to be adopted for successful management of technological changes in libraries;

i. Setting Objectives : An effective implementation of any IT application, the objectives of new systems should be clearly defined. Clearly stated objectives are the keys for successful IT Implementation. The objectives must be revised/ redefined and made as user oriented as possible. List the major and specific objectives for different sections of the library that will be accomplished through the use of technology. The objectives should be specific, realistic and easily measurable in quantitative measures. Well-defined objectives will form sound basis for effective strategic planning of financial resources, activities, processes, procedures and services. The objectives can include offering more efficient and effective delivery of current services or to add new services to help carry out the mission of the library.

ii. Assessment of Existing System : Introduction of new technologies in libraries is a major complex process, which requires through examination and analysis of various aspects & activities. Before introducing any new technology it is useful to do a formal study to investigate the existing system, find out the limitations, examine various options, and assesses the potential benefits of new technologies and identifies the needed resources for implementation of new technologies. The study collects the basic statistical information about collections, acquisitions circulations, services and users for complete description of the existing system. The assessment of existing system should involve collecting, organizing and analyzing facts about the current systems objectives, functions, processing operations, workflow, and size of files, inputs, outputs and resources. It surveys user needs in order to assess their expected services from a new system. User needs assessment can be done either through existing use patterns, interview, observation or surveys. The assessment should be done by a committee consisting of library staff, and computer specialists. Thorough assessment of the existing system will enable us to study and identify the requirements for the development of logical design of the new system.

iii. Identifying Priorities : Based on the information collected in the previous steps, it is necessary to determine which library functions should be automated and in what order of priority. In setting priorities, the factors considered include increased efficiency in manual operations, service improvements, high priority user needs and cost effectiveness. There are usually three factors that drive automation priorities in the typical library. 1) Manual processes that can be performed more efficiently using technology; 2) Services or service improvements that are a high priority for users 3) New services or service improvements that provide significant benefit in relation to cost. The functions most often automated include development of database, online public access catalogue (OPAC), acquisitions, circulation and serials control (Cohn, et al, 1998).

iv. Evaluation of Software Options : Having specified the functional requirements of a system, it is necessary to identify suitable hardware and software package. Software should be selected first which would ultimately decide about the type of hardware required. Software package is the most crucial for the success of library automation as it has many implications for a library's operations, services, staff and users. The success of library automation depends largely on the selection of right software and its effective implementation. Today, a wide variety of library software packages are available on the market. Selection of an appropriate package suited to a particular library and its intelligent implementation are challenging complex tasks in library automation process. Therefore, libraries should evaluate all the available options carefully in order to select the best possible option that can match both the priori: requirements and available financial resources. The various options available for library automation art' turnkey systems, stand alone or integrated systems, in-house developed systems and cooperative network systems. There are two types of library automation software: Standalone single function software and Integrated library software.

Standalone software is designed to use for anyone of the library functions. In the beginning, most of the libraries have initiated computerization with a single function. The systems designed for functions such as cataloguing, circulation, acquisition and serials control existed independently from each other and the exchange of data among the systems was not possible. Subsequently, due to limited facilities of stand-alone software and increasing capabilities of hardware, software, and communication technologies, integrated library automation software has emerged integrated software is one that computerizes multiplicity of library functions using one common database. In this system, all the library functions such as acquisition, cataloguing, circulation and serials control are integrated in such a way that they share common data and files. Integrated library software packages have become increasingly popular as they enabled libraries to computerize many functions and greatly contributed to the success of total library automation missions. These software packages overcome the problems of compatibility, prevent duplication of efforts, and improve efficiency in library operations, offers greater scope for staff savings and better provision for comprehensive management information.

v. Requesting Proposals : Once the decision to purchase integrated software is taken, it is necessary to request proposals from prospective vendors whose software's is considered to be potentially useful for the new system. The specifications of the required system form the basis for the formal request for proposal. It should clearly indicate all the mandatory and desirable functional, technical and performance requirements including the standard format used for submission of proposals. The proposals received in standard form facilitate to compare the functionality, cost, maintenance, support and all other features of software in a systematic and logical manner.

EVALUATING PROPOSALS AND SELECTION OF SOFTWARE

Once the proposals are received, they must systematically be evaluated preferable by a team consisting of library and computer professionals for selecting the best software for the library. The evaluation of proposals can be done based on the standard criteria which include software's functionality, usability, user-friendliness, compliance with specifications, cost, training, documentations, maintenance support, vendor's capacity for software updating/ up-gradation and past performance. The evaluation of proposals for selection of suitable software would be based on three basic criteria, functionality, and cost and vendor reputation. The sources of information for evaluating software include:

1. Reading journals and other references works.
2. Discussing with other librarians using the same software.
3. Personally visit and observe the actual working of software in successfully automated libraries.

4. Have informal discussions with potential software suppliers.
5. Invite prospective vendors to give demonstration on the software functional capabilities.

Based on the information collected from the responses, demonstrators, current users' experiences and other sources, the evaluation team reviews and evaluates the entire proposal using standard evaluation criteria and selects the software. Each proposal must be critically evaluated to make sure that all the essential mandatory functional requirements are met by the particular system so selected. After selection, the library needs to negotiate and sign the service contract with the vendor of software selected. Keep good relations with vendors and make maximum use of their full service support. They provide good in house training and help in data entry, migration and conversion.

IMPLEMENTATION AND OPERATION OF INFORMATION TECHNOLOGY

Implementation of new system involves various activities like site preparation, acquisition of furniture, testing of software, system conversion, data conversion, development of databases, bibliographic standards.

i. System Conversion : Planning for the shift from the existing system to the implementation of new system can take one of following approaches, depending on the size and complexity of the new system (Haravu, 1995). The followings library software packages are available in India namely, Alice for Windows, Basis Plus / Techlib Plus, LibSys, e-Granthalaya, Libsuit, DELPLUS, MINISIS, Sanjay, SOUL, Troodon, WINISIS, etc.

ii. Phased Implementation : In this, the new system is divided into sections. Each section is installed individually and only when it is considered to be operating fully satisfactorily, the next logical section will be installed. This method is suitable in situations where there are a large number of transactions.

iii. Parallel Implementation : In this, both the old and new systems are operated in parallel for a specified period of time until of the new system is performing satisfactorily. This method is adopted for complex systems.

iv. Pilot Implementation : In this, the system may be installed in a smaller scale, e.g., in a departmental library before it is installed in the main library. This way the problems of the new system can be better understood and tackled without upsetting a major area of operation. This is a useful approach for a multi-site environment.

v. Complete Changeover : In this, the old system is replaced by a new system on a specified day. This is feasible when the new system or application is relatively simple and there is not much preparatory work needed to replace the old system in one operation. The approach used for change over from existing system to new system depends upon several factors like system potential, type and size of library, financial, human resources available and time limits.

vi. Retrospective conversion : Retrospective conversion is a process of converting the library's total collection into computer readable bibliographic database. It is a costly, labour intensive and complex process. The most commonly used data conversion methods include data entry by the existing staff, hiring outside staff on contract basis and importing data from databases. Each of the methods has its own advantages and disadvantages. However, in practice a hybrid approach using combination of all the three methods may be adopted depending upon the situation, the size, nature and type of materials. The library's bibliographic database created through a retrospective conversion need to be effectively maintained subsequently incorporating needed changes like deletion and addition of titles. It is a large task and existing library staffs are busy with their regular duties, it is better and cheaper to hire temporary staff to enter data into the computer.

vii. Standards : Libraries planning for automation should adhere to standards in the development of databases.

Standards for description of bibliographic information in a database are essential for inter changeability and portability of files and to participate in networking for sharing of resources efficiently. Most of the Indian libraries are not being able to follow uniform standard formats while designing and developing in house databases. Each library follows its own formats there by giving a less scope for resource sharing and exchange of information. Communication, exchange of information and resource sharing will not be easily possible without uniform standard entries in a database. Standardization in the data elements, standard procedures of data entry and data storage are essential to ensure compatibility for interconnection, easy transfer of information and sharing of resources. Co-operation in exchange of information and resource sharing is easily possible only when there is uniformity in formats, structures of databases among the participating libraries. Developments of uniform technological standards are essential for standardization, networking, communication and sharing resources.

viii. Maintenance : Maintenance of infrastructure facilities like computers, Printers, UPS, air-conditioning needs to be given importance while planning for IT implementation. A provision should be made to see that all these machines must be in a working condition at all times. If computers and other equipment have to function properly, they should be protected from environmental hazards and power failure.

ix. Evaluation : Having used for considerable period of time after implementation, evaluation needs to be carried out to assess the extent to which new technology meets the goals and objectives set for it. Evaluation process helps to monitor progress toward the specific objectives and make necessary timely revisions responsive to new technological developments, products and opportunities. It is necessary that the library monitors IT activities, evaluates performance and tries to upgrade the existing technology or introduce new technologies. Evaluation has to be done periodically in order to assess the cost effectiveness of new services. The evaluation should include assessment of hardware utilization, staff and users perceptions about new system/ services and fulfillment of library's needs and objectives. Regular feedback from users and staff in the form of surveys, interviews and observations will help us to evaluate their satisfaction about new technology based services. Staff and users suggestions will be used as input for future improvements.

QUALITY PARADIGM OF EXCELLENCE IN LIBRARY SERVICES

The library services have changed very fast in the last twenty years and at the same time electronic resources, networks and the World Wide Web represent a large portion of the library services. The librarians must manage staff, information in several supports, and technical activities to produce quality services. Quality services means resources and services, which satisfy users' expectations and perceptions. It is very clear that librarians must use management tools to run the library services. These tools such as TQM, SERVQUAL, LibQUAL help them to assess services, to make decisions, to improve services and to achieve a better quality. The networked environment offers libraries' challenges and opportunities in a number of areas including management, services, and collection development. The library needs to describe and identify the issues meriting attention by the library professionals to gear up the library product and services so that user communities get satisfied coming to library. The libraries have transformed drastically from storehouses for books and journals to the powerhouses of knowledge and information since the middle of the 20th century. The information and communication technology is responsible for this revolution. The very existences of libraries are dependable on users' satisfaction. Users are getting satisfied when the library is able to rise to his or her expectation or meet the actual needs. A quality service is said to be one, which satisfy the users' expectation resulting a good experience. Throughout the history, libraries were mainly concerned with collection development and processing. The library professionals gave less concern to quality in product and services never checked whether the users are satisfied or not. The library being a service organization, its prime objective is to provide the right documents, information and services to its users. Only the users' satisfaction survey will facilitate the assessment of their satisfaction with products and services offered.

There are various methods, tools and techniques to measure, control and improve the quality of library services. Quality measurement and evaluation assumes great importance in modern libraries, as it brings immense benefits to the library as well as user community. Different methods like collection of data for measuring the performance and quality of libraries. The quality is "One that wears well, is well constructed will last for long time" and the strategic definition is "meeting customers' requirements." Juuran 'The quality is fitness for purpose' Robinson, "Quality is meeting the requirements of customer- now and in the future. Quality of a product or service is the ability of the product or service to meet the customers' requirements.

Quality Concept in Library Services : The library is an organization to offer reference and information services to its users. Library service is the combination of the services-process and its delivery. In a library, the service offered from acquisition section, technical section, maintenance section, etc. are the processes carried out there and thereafter delivered to the users. The quality starts from the acquisition section, which carried uniformly to circulation section. Therefore it is very necessary for librarian to understand the users, what they want, how they want, and when they want the documents and information.

Improvement of the Quality in Library Services: In this information age it is very easy to make a quality based library if the parent body or concerned authority assists financially as well as collectively. It is very necessary for the librarian and its parent body to look forward for the present and future generation to cope up with international phenomena. A user must be educated with proper technology to use the library effectively. He or she should have knowledge of what facilities and services are available in the library and information centre and how to access those efficiently and effectively. To improve the service quality the user satisfaction survey is a tool that provides both quantitative and qualitative data. It is an important part of libraries for process and performance measurement.

Main steps to measure users' satisfaction are conducting sample survey, data collection, process and analysis of data, Interpret and present the data and Finding out result. With the help of the result the librarian can take new steps for development of library. The regular survey will enable the library to understand the changes in user's satisfaction and to plan the services accordingly.

The users' satisfaction is based on many factors like : A source of up-to-date information, knowledge, accessing facilities and assistance. The library should organize its facilities visible to the users; otherwise they may not have it and get dissatisfied.

Accessibility : The library resources and services should be easily accessible. Books should be arranged in shelves in proper classified order, so that the users can locate books quickly. In case of electronic library the electronic database like OPAC will help the users to find out the books in stacks.

Tangibles: The tangibles of libraries, namely the building, furniture and other physical facilities, collection, staff, machines etc. should be sufficient and appropriate and useful for the users.

Courtesy / Friendliness : The library staff should be very courteous and friendly with the users.

Physical appearance / Atmosphere/ Cleanliness/ Comfort : The appearance of library, its facilities, collection, staff and services should be attractive and pleasant. A Welcoming atmosphere should be must. Furniture; floor, racks, documents etc. should be neat and clean.

Process- Reliability / Communications : The processing part of the library should be dependable and efficient that suffices the expectations of the users. The way of communication, assistance and guidance also greatly affect the satisfaction of the users.

Some useful criteria to measure users' experience in a library are: Speed of services delivery (Access time, location, processing, etc.). Value added services such as Xerox service, CAS, SDI etc. and Technology used. It is observed that if something goes wrong that can be very easily learned from the users, so the users' complaints can be taken as good measure of user satisfaction.

Steps for staff to meet the users' needs : Being responsible for the total service quality to the users both the Technical staff and frontline staff in the library should serve the users, Services must be provided to the users in a most effective way. Providing maximum benefits to the users form collection and facilities.

Stay close to users: Library cannot understand users' needs, tastes, interests etc. without listening to them, and services without users' interest will be a mere wastage. Users must be treated well, informed well and acknowledged well about the services to the users.

The five laws of Ranganathan help in quality improvement of service as those are concentrated to the users very seriously. The laws directly advocate towards libraries' collection development, speedy processing, maintenance and quick retrieval of information by users. The first law is a direction for measuring the quality of a library; quality in terms of contents, accessibility and availability as and when needed. The second law implies needs of users. In order to meet this law the library has to index all micro and macro documents so that every reader can find out his or her requirements. The third law implies the importance of book/ information selection in a library. The law advocates scientific document selection, subject based organization, advanced and in depth indexing, efficient and effective searching and locating tools, Staff assistance, open access, extension services, publicity programs, etc. The fourth law indicates the importance of fast and efficient services to the users with the advanced technologies, method, techniques and tools. Open access, digital services, classified arrangement of documents in shelves, location and directing guides, excellent searching tools, and techniques i.e. Online public Access Catalogue (OPAC) in an automated library, Xerox facility, Online Information services, qualified and experienced staff will ensure fast service to the users. Lastly the fifth law implies collection development, changing of all components of a library. Every day the world of documents and information is changing tremendously. Now the information is recorded not in papers alone, too many media, the latest are the electronic and digital form. So in today's world the library may called as information and knowledge house of world as a whole if it is supported by advanced information and communication technologies.

MEASURING QUALITIES OF LIBRARY SERVICES

The Total Quality Management (TQM) is one of the techniques used for the improvement and maintenance of quality or performance of the library. It is to provide the right information to the right users at the right place and time and also at the right cost. The most important components of TQM in a library are: Benchmarking, Performance Measuring and Monitoring and Qualification and experience of staff.

Benchmarking is a process of comparing the operations, products and services of a library with a library doing quality processes and offering quality products and services to the users. Performance measurement: is necessary to identify the problems, if any and find out new ways for improving the products or services. It requires both qualitative and quantitative data. The major performance indicators of the library functions are:

Acquisition : Efficiency, effectiveness, cost productivity.

Classification : Accuracy, Time factor, cost.

Cataloguing : Efficiency, time effectiveness.

Technical Processing : Efficiency, effectiveness, cost productivity.

Collection Management : Efficiency, ease, accessibility, effectiveness. Quality of service depends on quality and experience of staff. The TQM supports user education, sufficient and convenient technical infrastructures.

The SERVQUAL is the most popular assessment tool of service quality. It is designed by the marketing research team of Berry, Parasuraman, and Zeithaml. SERVQUAL evolve a set of five dimensions to assess the service quality.

Tangibles : Appearance of physical facilities, equipments, personnel, and communication materials.

Reliability : Ability to perform the promised service dependably and accurately; giving correct information asked.

Responsiveness : Willingness to help users and provide prompt service making new information available.

Assurance and empathy : Knowledge and courtesy of employees and their ability to convey confidence to users. It involves politeness, friendliness, skill to provide information.

Access : It means there are adequate staff and equipments as well as hours of operation. Location of library is central and convenient.

Communications: It involves understanding the users' needs precisely, provision of user education, teaching library skills to users, and the use of language understandable to different categories of users.

Security : It involves physical safety within the library, and keeping library dealings secured.

Liquid + is a library service quality measurement tool based on the SERVQUAL models of assessing service quality. It is standard survey instrument used in many libraries. It is a tool measuring users' perception of service quality and identifies gaps between desired, perceived and minimum expectation of services. LibQUAL +TM 2002 is the latest version to measure the quality of service.

Users' Expectations on Quality of Services : Modern building and furniture are required for a good library. A good library provides excellent facilities and services. Required books and journals in adequate number will be available with attractively displayed in a good library. In a good library, the staff will assist the users for locating a document. Accurate information and proper records will always be available in a good library. The staff of a good library will have sufficient knowledge to answer user's questions. Easy accessing and convenient working hour should have in a good library.

Users' Perception on Quality of Services : The users always perceive a Library as modern building and furniture, provides excellent facilities and services, available necessary books and journals in adequate number and displayed attractively, assists the users for locating the documents needed, keep accurate information and proper records, the staffs have proper knowledge to answer the question and easily accessible with convenient working hours.

FACILITIES IN A QUALITY BASED LIBRARY

i. Physical Facilities : Good library is easily accessible, good layout for a good library, sufficient space, lighting and ventilation, clean, tidy and hygienic and cosy and comfortable furniture.

ii. Library Collection : Good collection of textbooks, journals, reference books, online journals, e-books, etc. is needed in a good library, good library displays new arrival of books in separate shelves and good library offers open access to the collection.

iii. Library Staff : Staff in a good library should be experienced with knowledge of modern technology; staff should help the users to locate the documents needed and do their works in time and sufficient staff to run the library.

iv. Technical Processing : Good library acquire new documents in time, shelf arrangement and rectification is a never ending process in a good library, good library has proper catalogue or database for collection (OPAC etc.) and good library has prompt processing, charging and discharging system.

Today library introduces many new services either converting existing services into e- services or by developing and implementing entirely new services for searching, delivery and use of information. Such new or converted services include e.g. online service, portals, digitized collection, etc to enhance the quality of library services. Quality will be mainly defined by the speed and accuracy of reference and information delivery services, open access to both physical collection and online retrieval systems. The comprehensiveness and good support from library staff is most important needs in a library. The efficiency of background processes, convention of workshop, seminar, in service training of new technology introduced, refreshment course organized by library professional community are most essential for library to cope with globalization. Performance measurement and user survey can show whether a library is efficient and effective in delivering services. The Total Quality Management, Data collection and analysis of data, SERVQUAL, a scale for measuring service quality, LibQUAL, an instrument for measuring library quality are some methods and techniques to evaluate, control and improve the quality of a library. The greatest chance of success will come from affiliating the library with the unique goals of its parent organization.

EXCELLENCE IN LIBRARIES: A QUALITY ASSURANCE PERSPECTIVE

In its earliest days, the Library was characteristic of its time in being conservative, hierarchically structured and risk-averse. As the pace of technological change accelerated and expectations of services increased, it became apparent that change would be a constant, but often unpredictable, factor in the library and information environment. The Library executive recognised that an appropriate framework in which to manage constant change in all aspects of the business would be critical to future success and sustainability in an increasingly competitive environment, with wealthy, century's old, metropolitan libraries.

In the library world, excellence has traditionally denoted extensive collections, capacious facilities, sufficient staff and a service orientation. The first three attributes are largely resource-dependent. In the provision of service however, there appeared to be a clear opportunity to excel. Excellent service, it was believed, required excellent people and high quality, cost effective supporting processes and they are not only essential to the success of the university's researchers and students, but are of strategic importance in achieving the university's mission and goals." (McGregor, 2000).

In adopting the Excellence Framework, the Library not only sought to improve its performance in all areas but to measure and compare performance and outcomes with other organizations. The result was to demonstrate competitiveness with others and the primacy of the Library's role in assisting the University to achieve its goals, especially those aimed at the attraction and retention of students. The banner chosen for the introduction of the program was Quality Service Excellence.

ADOPTING AN EXCELLENCE FRAMEWORK

A framework assist in identifying further improvements as well as enabling effective management of the inevitable changes and developments mandated by external forces, such as the revolution in information and communication technologies. A quality excellence framework was seen as a model for organising and integrating initiatives and building on previous change interventions. Although accepted as a truism in change management theory, implementation of the theory through genuine involvement in planning, as opposed to the mere communication of information about plans, is probably less well accepted and practiced. Another insight was the need for extensive staff preparation. Skill development and educational opportunities for all staff are vital facilitating factors in any change effort. The potential of an organisation is realised through its people's enthusiasm, resourcefulness and participation." (ABEF, 2003). This principle was already internalised by the library executive as evidenced by the commitment to staff development and performance management established prior to 1994. The twelve principles are philosophically acceptable to the Library executive and, in essence, they comprise statements of good management practice. The disparate elements of effective management practice: human resources, industrial relations, customer relationship management, leadership strategies and planning processes are all integrated in a model underpinned by a systems approach and informed by systematic data collection, information and knowledge management. The principles of excellence are:

i. Clear direction allows organizational alignment and a focus on the achievement of goals.

ii. Mutually agreed plans translate organizational direction into actions.

iii. Understanding what clients' value, now and in the future, influences organizational direction, strategy and action.

iv. To improve the outcome, improve the system and its associated processes.

v. The potential of an organisation is realised through its people's enthusiasm, resourcefulness and participation.

vi. Continual improvement and innovation depend on continual learning.

vii. All people work in a system; outcomes are improved when people work on the system.

viii. Effective use of facts, data and knowledge leads to improved decisions.

ix. All systems and processes exhibit variability, which impacts on predictability and performance.

x. Organisations provide value to the community through their actions to ensure a clean, safe, fair and prosperous society.

xi. Sustainability is determined by an organisation's ability to create and deliver value for all stakeholders.

xii. Senior Leadership's constant role modeling of these principles and their creation of a supportive environment to live these principles, are necessary for the organisation to reach its true potential.

On reflection, the framework has been invaluable in maintaining a holistic perspective and in reducing preoccupation with technical and technological problems. As mentioned above, for reasons of competitiveness with other information providers and for positioning within the university, the Library sought benchmarks or performance indicators that would measure outcomes and overall organizational performance. These indicators would, desirably, be sufficiently robust to withstand close scrutiny by stakeholders and would enable the Library to compare itself with recognised 'best practice' organizations. Within the Library and information sector at the time, benchmarks and indicators to measure effectiveness as well as outcomes were difficult to find.

Libraries are different in that their main product, information, is not 'used up' when 'consumed' and does not usually generate a cash flow. They are 'public good' organizations. The value or return on investment delivered by libraries is of a social, educational, or cultural value and this is difficult to measure. Libraries are compared with other organizations in terms of functions and structures then the differences between profit and not for profit organizations appear, at least on the surface, to be minimal. Like corporations, libraries are required to manage budgets, and may generate a surplus, if not a profit. Their importance is reflected in the growth of management programs for librarians. Like other organizations, the impact of technological change has been pre-eminent in the last twenty years and management of information and communication technology consumes a large proportion of library leaders' portfolios. In recent years, concepts such as client relationship management, partnership management and promotion and marketing have assumed greater importance in libraries. Schwartzman (1995), students as customers such as recognising them "as participants in the educational process instead of passive recipients of whatever the institution decides to dish out" and concluded that the advantages are "outweighed by the dissimilarities between commercial transactions and education". Quinn (1997), in discussing the application of quality concepts in the non commercial setting of academic libraries, sees difficulty in defining the customer in an environment of many different potential customers such as students, faculty, administrators and parents, all of whom may have different expectations of the Library.

MANAGING THE CHANGE PROCESS

Knowledge and experience of quality management was identified as an essential competency for all managerial roles. Quality awareness is a core training requirement for all staff. Potential recruits and existing staff are thus aware of the continuing importance of this skills set. A change principle which found to be particularly effective follows: primary importance is that leaders should have realistic expectations of the length of time needed to implement and integrate an organization wide change, involving, quality program, cultural change, individual and team development and significant learning of new skills and knowledge. Identifying gatekeepers or change agents, those staff who are change-oriented and who are influential with other staff, is valuable in disseminating the message in more informal contexts. The importance of systematic communication cannot be overemphasised. Effective communication depends on the development of a variety of mechanisms, processes and actions, enabling the dissemination of consistent messages on a planned and regular basis. Successful internal communication is perhaps the most often criticised aspect of organizational management and the most difficult goal to achieve.

i. Rewards and Recognition : Leaders and gatekeepers alike should be encouraged to model the values and behaviours associated with the change effort. Recognising and rewarding active participants in the process provides visible symbols of the espoused values. Incentives to change, in the form of awards and other recognition are motivating for some staff. The question of performance related rewards in libraries is yet another challenge as rewards which are common in business organizations, such as bonuses, promotion and fringe benefits are not readily available to Library managers.

ii. Organizational Culture : In a climate of constant change, growing competition and expanded student expectations of services, organizational flexibility is paramount. Traditionally, libraries are highly structured, regulated and hierarchical with defined departmental boundaries. Perhaps library organization charts reflect the rule-based structure of cataloguing and classification systems and the adherence to codes essential to the effective retrieval of information. The TQM is the first managerial movement that has specifically considered culture and the values that develop in an organization" (Dawson and Palmer, 1995, p.55). The culture envisaged in TQM theory is one that supports flexibility, continuous change and commitment to organizational goals. The Library executive strongly believed that cultural alteration and improvement were both necessary and possible; and that they must accept responsibility for leading the change and for modeling the attributes and behaviours conducive to the envisaged culture.

iii. Benchmarking : Benchmarking is defined as: a method of comparing and measuring processes and outcomes with those of recognised leaders, with the intent of improving performance. Approach Thinking and planning.

- Identifies the organisation's intent, the thinking and planning it undertakes to design the strategies, processes and infrastructure to achieve the intent, including the design of performance indicators to track progress.
- Deployment 'Implementing and doing.
- Describes how strategies, structures and processes have been put into practice
- Results 'Monitoring and evaluating.
- Demonstrates how measures or achievement associated with the Approach are monitored and examines trends in performance.
- Improvement Learning and adapting.
- Examines what has been learned and how this learning is used to improve the approach and deployment.

iv. Success and Sustainability as Indicators of Success : The indicators of sustainability are concerned with the collection of information to predict likely future relevance and viability. The Library is widely regarded as the heart of the University, as a model of excellence in service and as possessing a 'different' culture. Acutely aware of the volatile and increasingly competitive environment in which we operate, and of the many risks involved in choosing one strategy over another, we intend to continue collection and analysis of all factors which impinge on our business so that choice and positioning is based on the best possible information.

Some of these benefits and insights have been delineated defining benefit is that the decision to embark on a quality program through adoption. There is confidence in the ability of the Library's staff, working together as well as in partnership with clients and stakeholders, to identify solutions to whatever challenges both the Library and its parent organization may face in the future. Application of the principles and the assessment dimensions: Approach, Deployment, Results and Improvement have encouraged a collective focus on the core competencies of the Library; that is, what the Library must do well for the achievement of its vision, mission and goals.

3

Impact of Information Technology in Libraries

The impact of information technology is enormous and global in its magnitude. It has become an integral part of all aspects of the library. It has a profound impact on library operations, information resources &, services, staff skills requirements and users expectations. Information Technology has virtually unlimited potential for variety if useful applications in libraries as it significantly contributes to the improved quality, increased productivity, more efficient operations, better resource sharing and more effective services to the users. The proper exploration of new technologies in library is no longer a matter of choice but a matter of survival in an era of rapidly changing technology and global knowledge society. Today the success of a modern library is increasingly dependent on the most effective utilization and strategic management of new technologies in libraries. The development of library automation has been well documented. Borgman views development in this area as having three stages of evolution: 1.Efficiency of Internal Operations, 2. Access to Local Library Collections, 3. Remote Access of Library Resources.

IMPACT OF INFORMATION TECHNOLOGY ON LIBRARY ACTIVITIES

Beginning in the 1970s, library professionals moved to include additional features into existing technology and extended functionality through purchase of software modules from "turnkey vendors". Often during this period, a library would center its decision on circulation control then add software modules to the existing hardware base that might support acquisitions, classification, cataloging, circulation, serials control, materials booking and other functions. Most of these applications served to extend and modernise existing procedures common among libraries. Today's applications of technology in libraries are more focused on information content and the end user and as such support the user directly in his or her quest to identify information resources. The routine functions of IT includes as follows:

a. Acquisition

Acquisition System is concerned with finding book selection sources, searching and selection of books required, placing of orders with a wide range of suppliers, keeping track of orders, receiving and recording of their receipt, settlement of invoices and maintaining detailed accounts of funds. Harbour (1994) made a comparative study on the flow charts of a highly simplified example of a manual and automated acquisition and cataloging system. He found that the number of steps in the computerized process can be reduced by roughly half. Automated system eliminates five tasks such as typing order records; filing order records; typing catalogue cards; filing catalogue cards and updating budget figures. Automation has had several important impacts on acquisitions:

i. Reduction of paper 'and filing costs
ii. Eliminate duplicate orders by checking an on-order file and the library's catalog
iii. Able to download MARC records at time of order which reduces time, costs, and occurrence of error

iv. Access to easy-to-use currency conversion tables

v. Management reports to monitor vendor performance

vi. Tools to .track the spending of the library's entire materials acquisitions budget

vii. Limited access to online reviews although this is improving each year.

b. Classification

Computerization provides the following benefits in classification: it helps the Classifier in the selection of isolate terms, grouping and arranging them in hierarchical sequence. Helps a classifier in synthesizing the class numbers, saves time by avoiding reference to the schedules of scheme for classification on and often, the constructed class number can easily be used as a query language in a typical retrieval system and improves accuracy and speed in classification.

c. Cataloguing

Library Cataloguing is one of the important functions, which link users' requirements to the documents in a library. Computerized catalogue is the most efficient tool in retrieving information about the documents in a library easily and quickly. Woods (1986) stated that in manual system, all cards had to be drafted, checked, typed, proof-read, corrected, sorted, filed and the filing checked. If any book is moved to a new location, withdrawn or lost, all the cards had to be found and corrected. A catalogue based on computer file needs only one amendment to correct all the entries and has various other advantages: Additional entries can easily be made, Catalogue can be cheaply reproduced (in microform) in as many copies as desired and distributed in machine readable form. According to Rowley (1993) computerized cataloguing system offers many benefits such as The catalogue record has become the central bibliographic record for the library management system as these records can also be used in other functions, Interchange of catalogue records has led to greater standardization, The availability of union catalogues has facilitated more effective inter library lending, co-operative acquisition policies, co-operative resource sharing activities, No filing or other routine catalogue maintenance is required of catalogues, Different catalogue formats can be chosen for different catalogue locations, Extracts from the main catalogue database may be printed or consulted online and The cataloguing procedure has become more structured, with a significant proportion of stock being processed quickly. Automating cataloging was the first step to create a library's machine-readable database around which other modules and services could be built. Reference, resource sharing, serials control, acquisitions, circulation control and collection development are all dependent upon the availability of the core-cataloging database. The availability of MARC records and linking computer terminals using telecommunications have allowed catalogers to share bibliographic cataloging records. Impacts of automation on cataloging are:

i. Change in workflow has a big impact on productivity.
ii. Management expectations set original cataloging rates.
iii. The cost of a cataloging record varies, depending upon the source.
iv. The Lower costs incurred by substituting Para-professionals for librarians.
v. More use of copy cataloging which helps to lower costs.
vi. Elimination of card catalogs and their attendant filing and maintenance costs.
vii. Z39.50 standard returns a MARC record to the requesting library. Some libraries are using this fact to add bibliographic records to their database instead of using the more traditional sources of cataloging records.

d. Circulation

It is very lengthy and consumes much of staff time in repetitive works in a conventional system. The use of technological devices such as computers, barcode scanners and its software in circulation helps in performing these routine operations easily and quickly. Academic libraries are the most suitable candidates for computerization of circulation-control systems as they frequently have high-volume of circulating transactions per day. Kumar (1987) stated that an automated circulation system should perform the following functions: Provide information on the location of the item on loan at the bindery, on reserve, being re-catalogued, etc., Give details of items on loan to a borrower, Record of reserves, alerting the library staff on return of a reserved item by a borrower and print a book available notice to the one reserved, Print recall notices for items on long-term loan, Renewal of loan, Alerting library staff about over-due items and printing of overdue notices, Calculation of fines, printing of the fine notices, recording receipt of fines and even printing of fine receipts, Calculation and printing of statistics of various types, Analysis of summary statistics, Provision for handling special categories of borrowers and special types of materials, Printing due date slips: automatically generating orders for lost books, and Provision for inter-library loan transactions.

Circulation being a major and most difficult activity that takes place on a large scale in library dealing with all the users has a high visibility factor. Computerization of this activity would have immediate impact on the users, as the benefits of automation would immediately be transferred to the users. Automated circulation systems were introduced libraries to the concept of using barcodes as a way to uniquely identify each item in the collection. Using barcode scanners at the circulation desk speeded up the checkout and check-in process. The net effect of an automated circulation system is improved control over the library's collection and increased staff productivity. No staffing increases are required to cope with increased circulation levels. The improved productivity means that libraries have not had to increase staff even in the face of increased demand for services.

i. Generating timely overdue notices means faster return of overdue items.

ii. Fine revenues go up. There is less discussion about library fines since the computer tracks the checkout, renewal, and return dates.

iii. Items lost through the circulation system are reduced.

iv. Patrons are usually able to view their own patron record, determine the status of a hold request, place a hold, and perform other activities remotely by using the library's Web-based OPAC linked to or integrated with the circulation module.

Some libraries have installed self-checkout machines to provide additional service points at the circulation desk. This reduces staffing requirements at the circulation desk.

e. Serial Control

Serials include periodicals, newspapers, annuals, journals, memoirs, proceedings, transactions etc., of societies and monographic series. Serials are distinguished from monographs by their ongoing nature. The continuing nature of serials subscriptions creates problems and makes it a complex process requiring a separate control system. Rao (1983) stated that an automatic serial control system should perform the following functions:

i. Ordering : Ordering new journals; Renewal/ discontinuation; Sending reminders; Receiving the journals,

ii. Reader Services : Preparation of a list of periodicals received; preparation of a list of periodicals cancelled; Preparation of a list of holdings: List of holdings with their status (i.e., on shelf, in binding. in circulation etc.) and

iii. Management Services : keeping track of amount spent on Subscriptions, binding, estimation of the budget for the next year; Announcement of the missing serials for recording the same.

Managing serials is an important task that can consume significant staff resources in a non-automated setting. The ordering, renewal, invoicing, check-in, claims, binding, and dealing with cancellations are .all processes that require attention to details. While a majority of systems support the receipt of journal issues and allow the library to define a variety of arrival predication patterns, few systems support the MARC Format for Holdings at both the detail and summary holding levels. Among the benefits of automating serials are:

i. Increased control over receipt of issues. This allows the journal issues to get into the hands of the end user sooner. It also allows for the more timely and accurate claiming of issues that do not arrive.
ii. Production and maintenance of routing lists.
iii. Production of local, regional, and state serial holding lists.
iv. Management reports about the usage of each serial title.

Benefits Associated with Integrated Library System : The past two decades have seen a great deal of change in ICTs resulting in significant impact on information resources, human resources, financial resources, nature of service provision/delivery, user community, and authorities' attitude. Information technology has had a clear and persuasive impact in almost every area of the library be it the online catalog used by a library customer, in technical services, or in administrative services. There are several possible benefits that may accrue to a library as the result of using network and information technologies. These benefits will vary depending upon the functional area and how well the library has revised its manual procedures and processes to complement the automated system. Among these possible benefits associated with integrated library system are:

i. Improved Productivity : Existing staff members are able to cope with increased workloads or take on additional responsibilities, or both, as the result of the library having installed an integrated library system.

ii. Reduce Staff : In a few cases; libraries were able to reduce staff that was involved with labor-intensive, manual processes with high volumes of activity once the integrated library system had been installed. However, for a majority of libraries, there has been little or no reduction in the number of overall staff as the result of automation.

iii. Reduce Unit Cost of Operation : The efficiencies that can be achieved with an integrated library system allow a library to reduce the costs associated with a particular activity. For example, sharing cataloging data through a bibliographic utility such as OCLC allowed libraries to avoid duplicating the effort associated with creating original cataloging records. This reduced the number of professional staff and resulted in delegating work to lower-skilled and lower-paid staff.

iv. Improve Control : An integrated library system will accurately record the status and location of all items that are maintained in its database. Thus rather than having silos of paper records found only in one department, the online system allows every staff member to learn about and update information associated with a particular item or record.

v. Reduce Errors : Using an integrated library system means that the number of errors that would have occurred in a manual system are significantly reduced because the majority of systems use barcode scanners to uniquely identify an item.

vi. Improve Speed : Using an automated system means that a variety of activities are completed in a timelier manner. For example, materials are getting on the shelves faster circulation-related transactions happen quicker, and so forth.

vii. Improved access : Because the majority of library staff members have desktop workstations that are connected to the integrated library system, they each have access to the latest information about an item or record. In addition, the integrated library system will typically provide several indexes to the library's database (e.g. keyword indexes) that are not available with manual systems.

viii. Increase Range and Depth of Service : An integrated library system, especially a system that is accessible via the Internet, allows the library's customers to access the library's collection and other information resources 24 hours a day, 7 days a week. In addition, most systems will allow library patrons to view portions of their record, place holds, or be alerted when an item is available. Thus, the library patron is no longer constrained to visiting the physical library in order to receive services.

ix. Facilitate Cooperation : The ability of an ILS to export standard MARC records allows libraries to participate in various cooperative projects (building local, regional, and state databases; lists of serials owned by participating libraries; and so forth).

x. By-Products : An ILS allows a library to examine, by using a variety of historical statistical data gathered by the automated system, the range and quality of services it provides to its customers. For example, some libraries have examined the actual usage of its collection in an effort to understand the needs of its customers better.

IMPACT OF INFORMATION TECHNOLOGY ON LIBRARY SERVICES

There is no doubt that the technology in particular computers and ICT have made the most impact on libraries in areas that require the rapid and accurate storage and processing of structured data the ability to operate for 24 hours a day, seven days a week and worldwide connectivity and communication. Evans (2000) identifies key areas of recording stock (cataloguing) and its movement (circulation) as those most affected by technological change. Continuing the discussion Evans states that the next step is that of 'seamless inter-lending of material, utilizing the strengths of developing standards and faster and more efficient technologies. Hyde (1997) suggests that in the future, staff will work, not in a physical library, but elsewhere with all electronic access to collections.

Debowski (1999) highlights the following key factors in his study:

1. Significant advances in technology and increasing costs of journals and other print resources- massive growth in electronic services.
2. Budgetary maneuvers staffing pared down to essential levels so that infrastructure services may be developed.
3. Decreasing numbers of library visitors. Reduced coverage of service points sustaining basic services whilst offering extended electronic access.
4. Outsourcing- Argument for a more cost effective system.

Orenstein's (2006) paper traces the history of technology movement in library field and discusses in detail the impact of technology on library functions. Few of observations and findings on impact of technology are listed below:

1. Till ten years ago, libraries were book focused institutions. Library acquisitions, cataloguing and circulations were done via or managed by using print ledgers, pens and cards. Spreadsheets, databases or other s/w was never used to manage library data.
2. The first major wave came with the advent of digital storage and network technology.
3. In early 1990s Public Access Terminals and OPAC became ubiquitous to share information on library holdings. The access was PC-based. Access to holding to the outside world was not shared.

4. In 1990s CD-ROMs were invented and used to store large data which were inserted into single use PCs. In other words stand alone versions were prevailing.
5. In late 1990s Internet became life blood of information sharing not just for libraries, but for commerce, education, government and general public. High speed networking availability facilitated instant transfer of both text and graphics from one server to another. Storage and access issues eliminated, yet it free for everyone to place anything on WWW resulting in false information.
6. While Internet is a wonderful thing it is not a substitute for campus library or librarian. Librarian guide users how to find information whether print or online.
7. Rate of distance users increased exponentially challenging librarians to make many resources available online.
8. The role of academic librarian in the academic age is to promote access to accurate information to users. However, this role became more complex with information age.
9. It is important to note that even with all technical complexity and additional responsibilities, the librarians' core role as gatekeeper of information is unchanged.
10. Information searching, preparation of teaching materials, answering queries via technology is the great impact of Internet age.
11. The card catalogue replaced with web-based interface as a result the maintenance information was to be handled by technically competent support staff with accurate information. The typographical errors on card catalogues were widely noticeable online. It was also important to note, the online catalogue made accessible anywhere as it is web-based.

12. The library staffs were identified as knowledge workers.
13. One cannot have good education without libraries, and one cannot have good library without good library staff.

Schatz and Chen (1999) point that the public awareness of the net as a critical infrastructure in 1990s has spurred the new revolution of technologies for information retrieval in digital libraries. Further they say that digital libraries are a form of information technology in which social impact matters as much as technological advancement. Cairncross (1997) explaining the speed of Internet and remote access highlighted the death of time and geographical barrier. Further, the open search engines like Google, Yahoo etc. have become all-time powerful search tool for information seekers across the globe.

a. In-House Databases

Libraries are experiencing a significant impact of IT on information processing, sources and services. Rapid technological developments enabled libraries not only to improve the quality of existing services but also to offer a wide range of new services to users. Libraries use IT to create in-house databases of their holdings. Computerised databases provide easy and user-friendly access to the information resources and sound foundation for efficient information services. One of the fundamental characteristics of computer based information retrieval is that the database at the heart of the system may be used as the basis for a plethora of different products ranging from CD-ROM, through online access on an external host to printed indexes and current awareness bulletins.

b. Online Public Access Catalogue (OPAC)

The impacts of automated technology on the library patron using an OPAC, online databases, and reference services will be explored prior to examining the implications in technical services. The OPAC in the early 1980s, several studies have been conducted to identify the problems encountered by OPAC users, as well as to make suggestions for improving the OPAC experience (Matthews, Gary, and Ferguson, 1983) & (Matthews, 1986). Initially there were three main benefits that resulted when an OPAC was introduced into a library. These benefits included:

- ***Reduced costs*** to provide a library catalog No more filing cards because the largest component of the average library's budget is for personnel costs, eliminating the time it took to maintain and file cards in the library's card catalog resulted in significant savings. These cost savings accrue to the library on an annual basis, although this is frequently overlooked by a number of library managers and funding decision makers.
- ***Improved access to the collection*** : The OPAC provides not only was card catalog-like browse indexes (left-to-right, character-by-character); it also provides keyword indexes, often with Boolean limiting capabilities. In some cases even more sophisticated search tools, such as automatic synonym searching were also provided to patrons. As the World Wide Web spread through the 1990s, libraries moved to provide local dial-in modem access. Thus library patrons now had around the clock access to the library's collection from their home, office, or dormitory.
- ***Immediate access*** to location and status information given the remote access to the library's collection and other information resources, one of the real benefits for the patron is being able to determine whether an item of interest can be found on the shelves or if it is checked out or missing. This allows the patron to discover the status of an item before making a trip to the library.

c. Reference Services

Online catalogs may have started displacing physical

card catalogs in the 1980s, but mediated online searching typically performed by reference librarians was added to extend not replace the print collection. CD-ROM workstations and locally loaded databases that were added in the 1980s were intended to complement the resources available in the library. There after came the increase in Internet use in the 1990s and the access to online databases and other information resources that it provided. These newer technologies seldom replace the technologies already in place but more often are likely to coexist with those prior services (Tenopir, and Ennis, 1998).

Today reference librarians have access to the Internet and a variety of other information resources. Yet these highly trained professionals are called upon to help users cope with technology-from formatting a diskette, fixing printer paper jams, restoring frozen workstations, explaining rank order retrieval systems and so on. Lipow (1999) suggests that there are four trends contributing to instability in the reference environment:

1. As Internet use increases, use of reference services in the library decreases.
2. Many patrons feel that they don't need a librarian due to the Internet.
3. Reference librarians can't keep up with all of the new Internet resources that are appearing daily.
4. Commercial services are providing satisfactory information resources at the end user's point of need.

Some libraries have begun providing reference services through some electronic means-e-mail, chat, instant messaging, or submitting a Web form-rather than in person or over the telephone. The experience of libraries providing these new reference services suggests that, while the demand is not heavy, library patrons are satisfied with the service.

The bottom line is that the Internet changes the scope and dynamics of reference services and allows the library to provide an information portal that leads in and out of the library. In a collaborative environment the range and quality of reference services is no longer constrained by the size of a library's reference collection or the subject expertise of its reference staff.

d. Inter Library Loan

Inter Library Loan system deals with the process of borrowing items from other libraries. Development of ILL system has been relatively slow in India as compared to western countries due to lack of access to catalogues of other libraries collections in manual system. Now it is gaining momentum due to present library conditions with improved technological capabilities and network developments. Typically computerized Inter Library Loan system offers the following benefits: (Rowley, 1993) improved ILL transaction control and management, Off line preparation and storage of messages, Elimination of filing, searching, sorting and preparation of reports, Reduction of staff time required to process ILL requests, Enter the requests and the computer will create the forms and keep track of all the details of all records, Easy to download and upload [LL records, Update ILL records automatically by entering record numbers, Print downloaded ILL records using flexible formatting options, Maintains data, generate forms and produce various reports.

Rather than requiring a library customer to fill out a manual form that is submitted to a library staff member for review and follow-up action, some libraries have found that patron-initiated interlibrary loan requests using an automated system provides better service and lower costs. When evaluating interlibrary loan services, four factors are usually considered: What types of requests are being made (by subject area)? What is the fill rate (what proportions of requests are actually filled)? What is the service level (time from request being made to the library receiving the item)? What does the service cost? Interlibrary loan costs are not inexpensive. The lending library can photocopy an article and deliver it directly to the patron or library using a delivery service, fax, e-mail, Ariel, or snail mail. The net impact for the patron is that he or she receives the article in a matter of days rather than weeks.

Developing Library Network (DELNET) formerly Delhi Library Network has been actively engaged with the compilation of various Union Catalogues of the resources available in member-libraries. It has already created the Union Catalogue of Books, Union List of Current Periodicals, Union Catalogue of Periodicals, CD-ROM Database, Database of Indian Specialists, Database of Periodical Articles, Union List of Video Recordings, Urdu Manuscripts' Database, Database of Theses and Dissertations, sample databases of language publications using GIST technology and several other databases. DELNET is offering inter-Library loan and Document Delivery Services to its member libraries. ILL requests can be registered online for books. For the resources not available in the union catalogues and journal articles, requests can be sent to DELNET through E-mail. DELNET has also prepared ILL Guidelines for use by the member-libraries. The services are quite popular among the member-libraries (DELNET, 2011).

e. Online Database Search

Online database searching is one of the most important services and a powerful information searching tool for it can search millions of records in just a few minutes, thereby saving researchers and academicians days and weeks of manual searching. On-line Search Service refers to the mounting databases on a computer and making necessary arrangements for such databases to be searchable from a large number of remote user terminals. Some of the major database hosts are: DIALOG, DATA-STAR, ESNIRS, QUESTEL, STN international, ORBIT search service etc. The advantages of online searching over manual include speed, currency, convenience, access. ability to combine concepts and search elements to do both more complex searches and more specific searches, ability to modify the search strategy immediately.

The database industry is one that is strong and growing. Vendors provide access to a variety of data-text, numeric, images, sound, and video files. Database producers who create and provide these databases might be the primary publisher or a secondary publisher. Secondary publications include citations, abstracts, or other materials descriptions created by the primary or original publisher. In some cases, several databases are gathered together by a database distributor (e.g., Lexus/Nexus, ProQuest, EBSCO, GALE or Dialog). In other instances, a database is only accessible via the primary publisher. Traditionally, librarians have provided a value-added service by providing search intermediation services. Currently, end users seek direct access to these resources, which are often licensed by the library for use by its customer base.

When an online database publisher or distributor creates and maintains a database, it provides a value-added service that is involved with creating, editing, indexing, distributing, and archiving the database. The traditional distribution channels used by online database publishers are evolving with the availability of the Internet. Some publishers and database distributors are exploring how to provide direct end user access to the database, bypassing the library. Most libraries are moving away from subscribing to a database via CD-ROM and are moving to providing access via the Internet. Few of these databases support Z39.50 interoperability, although each year more publishers are starting to support this standard. In many cases, access to the online database is not well integrated into the library's OPAC and users must learn a new interface for each database they use. In addition, each database supports a unique set of controlled vocabulary terms and search syntax, which adds some complexity for the user who is conducting a search. Keyword searching dominates, and the majority of searches by end users are simple.

Increasingly, publishers are providing access to the full-text contents of their journals in electronic format, sometimes called e-Journals. In some cases, libraries are eliminating some of their print journals and relying on electronic access. For OPAC users, this means that they now have the opportunity to do full-text searching on the contents of these journals rather than relying solely on citations and abstracts. While the subscription cost per journal title is less than the printed version, there are a variety of other cost impacts for a library to consider. Typically, access to a specific set of e-Journals is bundled with other e-Journals, so the library may actually increase access to the number of journals for their end users.

The university libraries in India rely mostly on INFLIBNET, which provides abstracts and sometimes full text online free of cost to users. They also use other free online services provided by organizations like the National Information Systems for Science and Technology (NISSAT), the Council of Scientific and Industrial Research (CSIR) and UNESCO, as well as the World Wide Web.

f. CD-ROM Database Search

Optical discs, specifically in the form of CD-ROMs, became increasingly used as a medium for storage and dissemination of information during the 1990s. CD-ROMs provide a means of access to information as an alternative to online access to external databases via telecommunications networks, including the WWW. All six university libraries had acquired CD-ROMs during the past six years for the purpose of enhancing research and scholarly communication. However, they have been using basic standalone workstations that provide a single user with access to a single disc. With improved network connectivity in progress and with local area networks (LAN) in consideration, soon the issue of one user using one disc alone will come to an end since the LANs will be in place. Optical discs have become increasingly important as a medium for the storage and dissemination of information during the early 1990s. Optical discs represent alternative means of accessing information to online commercial databases.

O'leary (1990) stated that using CD-ROM databases at the point of use or in the library was found to have considerable effect on budget in a number of academic institutions and in one case CD-ROM virtually replacing online searching. This is particularly applicable to academic institutions, because of the high customer base, fairly predictable fixed type of demand and the frequent requirement for historical rather than current information.

Akeroyd (1991) observed that, since the installation of CDROM network at South Bank polytechnic library, demand has been so great that within three months, file server access had to be doubled. It has been found that its use has significantly reduced online expenditure, and led to a substantial increase in the number of interlibrary loans from students.

Biddiscombe (1991) stated that the networking of CD-ROMs is now being run successfully in a number of academic institutions. CD-ROM based information service has created positive benefits for the image of the library as a provider of information. The bibliographic database on CD-ROM will alert users to documents, whose existence they would not otherwise have suspected. This may lead to fuller exploitation of existing library resources and more demand for documents that can be acquired via library networks and inter library Joan (Rowley, 1993).

Smith (1993) reported that 82% of academic institutions used CD-ROMs and found them invaluable for end-user searching. All respondents generally agreed that CD-ROM searching was far more relaxing and far more fun than online searching. CD-ROM has a number of advantages over online. There is no telecommunication charges, costs are known in advance. It is intended for the end user and consequently can save staff time. Users do not have to worry about generating high bills through lengthy or complex searches or simply practicing searching techniques and downloading is generally easier.

g. Internet Service

Internet is a network of hundreds of computer networks spanning around the world. Internet has being vast information source enable libraries to provide a variety of information services to users. Innovative use of Internet technologies enable us to reach both local and distant users much more easily and effectively than hitherto possible. In addition to bibliographic and catalogue information, we can extend information content to cover full text, images, animations and full multi-media (Ressler and Trefzger: 1997). Rajasekhar (1998), the applications and services a librarian can provide on the Intranet and the Internet may include catalogue databases, current awareness bulletins, externally purchased databases, CD-ROM databases, remote information services, internal newsletters, reports and journals, and Internet information sources.

h. E-Mail and E-Bulletin

Electronic mail (e-mail) is the most common application used on Indian networks and is a popular and outstanding method of communication, particularly in workplaces, as both staff and users can correspond faster and more easily with each other. An Electronic Bulletin Board system is equally a very important source of information where users can leave messages of interest to a particular community of online users. Electronic Conferencing (EC) involves capabilities that take e-mail and bulletin boards a step further and makes online conversations possible. The Internet and the World Wide Web have passed over the walls of knowledge and through it the globe has become a small village. It has become an indispensable resource for academic libraries globally in helping them to enhance collections and improve services and operations. The World Wide Web provides the following information (Fecko, 1997) social, scientific and technical information (current research, abstracts of papers, etc.) popular culture and entertainment opinions PR-type company information; and many others.

These tools have become an acceptable and almost indispensable part of the work of academic libraries. The Internet, and especially the facilities it provides for access to electronic journals, has reduced the problems faced by researchers and academics of not being able to find consistent and up-to-date journals in the library due to heavy budget cuts.

i. Web 2.0 in libraries (Social Networking and Blogs)

Before blogging became popular, digital communities took many forms, including Usenet, commercial online services such as GEnie, BiX and the early CompuServe, e-mail lists and Bulletin Board Systems (BBS). In the 1990s, Internet forum software, created running conversations with "threads." Threads are topical connections between messages on a virtual "corkboard." The Blogs concept arrived in the 1990s. Blogs were originally named Weblogs, a name coined by Jom Berger in December 1997. This was later shortened to "Blog" with the person keeping the Web log being known as a "blogger", Blogs are usually maintained by an individual with regular entries of commentary, descriptions of events, or other material such as graphics or video. Entries are commonly displayed in reverse-chronological order. Blog can also be used as a verb, meaning to maintain or add content to a blog. Many blogs provide commentary on a particular subject; others function as more personal online diaries. A typical blog combines text, images, and links to other blogs, Web pages, and other media related to its topic. The ability of readers to leave comments in an interactive format is an important part of many blogs. "Blogs are a natural for librarians", says Paula 1. Hane (2001); certainly some librarians have been quick to recognize that Weblogs can be important sources of information and information dissemination tools for communication.

1. Library blogs : Blogs are perfect for dissemination of information as the system of dated entries makes it easy for viewers to identify new content. A number of the system's libraries have caught the fever as well. The growth of library weblogs has noticeable growth during last several years. In 2003 there were only 57 library weblogs, while in 2004 the numbers increased to 198 weblogs (Clyde, 2004). This number has reached up to 392 in the year 2006.

(Karami and Oloumi, 2006). Doug and Vogel (2003) have described a weblog project in an academic library to deliver information about library news, services and resources to the science faculty and students at Georgia State University, they developed a blog. Caver (2003) lists several public libraries that are using blogs to publicize news and events, while Harder and Reichardt (2003) suggest that academic libraries can develop department or subject specific weblogs to reach faculty and graduate students with content customized to meet their information needs.

Clyde (2004) has also investigated library weblogs in the late 2003; her findings show that public and academic libraries were more likely to have a weblog than other types of libraries. The most common aim or purpose was to provide news, information and links to Internet resources for library users. Few provided interactive facilities, and when provided, there was little evidence that the facilities were used to any extent. Only one-fifth of the weblogs are updated within the last day and only half within the previous week. It is interesting to note that less than half provided an RSS feed. The libraries may use the blogs because of:

i. Some provide up-to-date information on local events, fulfilling their role as a news and information source for their community. Others provide library news (both local and national), advocating for the importance of library support.

ii. Still others are using blogs to provide announcements of new library acquisitions, promoting the services that they work so hard to provide.

iii. And then there are those who are doing all these things at once!

iv. Direct users to useful, new or interesting resources;

v. Comment on local and national events and activities in the IT, book and library worlds;

vi. Provide news from the library/information service; and

vii. Request feedback or comments and generally help the library to engage with its users, especially those who rarely if ever visit a physical library.

As far as the advantages of blogs in libraries are concerned, they can be used in following ways:

i. In current awareness service, blog can be used to highlight news or resources of interest; and to post book reviews from students, faculty and the staff members;

ii. It list out the new acquisitions and to announce the library news and events. Using of systems such as RSS technology is another blog application in libraries for selective dissemination of information.

Librarians and information professionals, including those working in libraries and information centers, have begun using blogs to share ideas with colleagues and solicit feedback through the comments function. Blogs reflect a personal viewpoint, they allow readers to respond and comment. These 'give and take' fleshes out blog content and results in a sense of community among the participants.

2. Social Networking : A social networking service is an online service, platform, or site that focuses on building and reflecting of social networks or social relations among people, who, for example, share interests and/or activities. A social network service essentially consists of a representation of each user (often a profile), his/her social links, and a variety of additional services. Most social network services are web based and provide means for users to interact over the Internet, such as e-mail and instant messaging. Online community services are sometimes considered as a social network service, though in a broader sense, social network service usually means an individual-centered service whereas online community services are group-centered. Social networking sites allow users to share ideas, activities, events, and interests within their individual networks. The main types of social networking services are those which contain category places means to connect with friends (usually with self-description pages) and a recommendation system linked to trust. Popular methods now combine many of these, with Facebook and Twitter widely used worldwide, and other social networking are Nexopia, Bebo, VKontakte, Hi5, Hyves, Draugiem.lv, StudiVZ, iWiW, Tuenti, in, Nasza-Klasa, LinkedIn, Orkut, etc.

Social networks are also being used by teachers and students as a communication tool. Because many students are already using a wide-range of social networking sites, teachers have begun to familiarize themselves with this trend and are now using it to their advantage. Teachers and professors are doing everything from creating chat-room forums and groups to extend classroom discussion to posting assignments, tests and quizes, to assisting with homework outside of the classroom setting. Social networks are also being used to foster teacher-parent communication. These sites make it possible and more convenient for parents to ask questions and voice concerns without having to meet face-to-face. The advent of social networking platforms may also be impacting the ways in which learners engage with technology in general. The use of online social networks by libraries is also an increasingly prevalent and growing tool that is being used to communicate with more potential library users, as well as extending the services provided by the individual libraries.

j. Mobile Phone/ Wireless Service : Wireless phone application services that have been used in educational field are information queries and deliveries via SMS. Some WAP applications have been observed especially in the European countries. The University of Northumbria UK, for instance, has been providing campus wide information and various other administrative services to the respondents through

WAP services. Wireless application in higher education is projected to move beyond the basic services. The services, with the availability of WAP and high-speed wireless technology such as 3G, would allow for more advanced application such as E-learning, information retrieval and various online library information services. Wireless technology has the potential to offer many new possibilities for accessing information from online catalogues, online databases, the internet and virtual libraries. Among the wireless technologies includes digital cellular technologies, packet radio and wireless local area networks. Today, the convergence of mobile phones and the internet through the WAP standard presents libraries with a real opportunity to deploy wireless phone technology to manage their operations for the following services:

i. checking records of books borrowed;
ii. getting alerts on overdue books;
iii. getting alerts on outstanding fines;
iv. receiving reminders to return library items that will be due soon;
v. renewing library items;
vi. reference enquiry services;
vii. receiving text alerts to new resources on the library web site;
viii. getting alert on library event information;
ix. getting information from the library OPAC /database; and
x. Contacting librarian for help.

Currently, libraries are looking for ways to communicate with their users in such an effective manner. Wireless application in library services can be established through an infrastructure that integrates the library systems and databases, through an application system that allows for information to be processed and delivered to a smaller device such as a mobile phone unit (Karim, 2006).

IMPACT OF INFORMATION TECHNOLOGY (IT) ON LIBRARY STAFF

Human resources are the key to the successful use of any technology in a library. The greatest challenge faced in the deployment of IT is the development of skilled human resources. Staff who can support and comply with the computer and network environment is essential for effective IT implementation. Positive attitudes and actions of staff involved in IT use are regarded as crucial for the successful implementation of a new system. The attitudes of library staff members toward a proposed automation project fall into fairly distinct categories. Fortunately, for the sake of progress toward automating libraries, the great majority of staff members are open-minded, reasonable and enthusiastic people who show a genuine interest in learning more and being included in training and orientations. A second group exhibits attitudes ranging from indifference to hostility. Some of these employees, driven by fear or a strong preference for the status quo, are truly resistant to automation. They may have an irrational fear of technology (Walton, 1982).

Luquire (1983), 'to deal with the new technology and maintain balance between human considerations and the technology of library automation, better understanding of the complexities of the perceptions and attitudes of people is mandatory. Most of the process of human and organizational management is at the mental and psychological plane rather than the physical. Shaw (1986) Staff feels happier if they are consulted in the automation process and kept informed of developments. A year after automation, he found that staff felt that services were better and faster than before. Much research has suggested that the style of implementation and consultation with the workforce is more significant in gaining employee acceptance of new systems, than actual changes in the jobs themselves. Kiesler, et al. (1987) found that there was even segregation between those who worked -on the automation project and those who did not. Hence a new social order is being established in some libraries with different people gaining rewards, recognition and influential power for their technological skills. There was evidence of some ill feeling about this from the other staff. Klerk and Euster (1989) found that the technical services staff, accustomed to the detail and specificity required by a computer are adapting easily. Prince and Burton (1998) found that senior academic-related staffs were largely disinterested in technology, the more recently qualified staff being more positive adopters of innovation. According to Dobb (1999), without a very committed and energetic staff willing to share their skills and enthusiasm for library work with our patrons and with each other every day, our organization could not really progress in using technology.

Staff Training : Most often, emphasis is placed on the hardware and software aspects of the technology without giving due importance to staff training and development that is needed to ensure effective use of potential of technology. Training library personnel and providing facilities of hands on experience in using computers are important aspects to be given serious consideration. Continuous training on emerging technologies is necessary to develop, maintain and improve skills, knowledge and competencies. An intensive need-based practical oriented training should be imparted to library personnel to instill confidence in order to handle and manipulate new technologies. Further, the staff may also be deputed to libraries, which are in advanced state of automation for gaining knowledge and hand-on experience in using IT.

One of the most important factors for successful implementation of information technology is the level of competence of the staff (Hofmann, 1995). One of the major problems in effective use of information technology in libraries is the shortage of technically skilled and competent manpower. Without adequate knowledge, staff members working at computers have to spend a lot of time for learning, experimenting and using IT applications in real situations.

Staff members feel that these rapidly changing technologies actually interfere with their job. Further, it is found that the staff experience increased techno stress as a result of attending to both routine as well as automation works simultaneously. Working knowledge of IT in library personnel is fundamental for its successful implementation in library. IT has immense potential for handling various library functions. To make full use of this potential in library management, it is essential that the library should have adequate personnel who have thorough knowledge of IT applications in libraries. But in practice, most of the library personnel do not have adequate level of knowledge and competence of IT applications in libraries. Working knowledge can be gained only when one is given an intensive training and gets practical hands on experience in using IT.

IT is one of the most rapidly changing areas in the library environment. Keeping up with changes and trends in library technology involves several tactics. The important include: Arrange short term training courses for staff on library automation, databases, LAN, Internet and other timely needed current topics, Arrange staff visit to successfully automated libraries, Attending professional meetings, conferences and seminars, Reading professional literature, Personal contacts with experienced fellow professionals, Brochures of new software packages, products and services, Participation in professional news and discussion groups and Subscription of mailing lists

Staff Involvement : Staff acceptance is another important factor contributing to the successful use of IT in libraries. The new technologies will be successfully implemented without the acceptance, full support and commitment of all levels of library staff. It is a human tendency to resist change. As some of library staff still lacks knowledge of IT, they are not convinced of the use of IT and so not willing to respond positively to the change of new technologies. There is also a psychological fear in the minds of the library staff that the use of IT in libraries may lead to retrenchment/unemployment. It should be made clear to the staff that IT is used to introduce new services and make improvements and not to reduce either the existing library services/employees. Further they must be convinced that the rapid spread of IT use will lead to a tremendous demand for skilled personnel. Therefore, they must be assured that no one is going to loose his job as a result of the introduction of IT in libraries. The success of use of IT in library depends on the extent to which supervisory and operational staffs are involved in its planning, design, analysis and implementation. The psychological barriers to change must be cleared in the initial stage involving all the staff in its implementation. Staff involved in IT implementation project need to be trained and must be made aware of the latest developments.

Staff Size : According to Johnson (1991) a number of automated libraries show that non-professional staff arc the group most likely to have their numbers reduced by the implementation of a new system. Nearly half (48.2 per cent) of the participants reported a decrease in the number of non-professional or 'clerical' positions as a direct result of automation.

Jones (1999) stated that a large majority of the total respondents report reductions of personnel in all categories - support staff, librarians, and student workers. There was a definite decrease in the number of support staff at each library where these surveys were distributed. However, 57 percent of respondents do not believe technology is responsible for most of the personnel changes. In all three libraries, the largest percentage of respondents (i.e., 53 percent, 68 percent, and 55 percent) said that technology was not responsible for most of the personnel changes. Horny (1987) stated that automated systems frequently bring with them opportunities for redesigning the way in which people work as well as in the structure of the whole organization. Certain jobs may no longer be significant. Others may combine, or become interdependent, due to the way in which functions interrelate within the system. He documents technical services staff reallocations at Northwestern University, with work responsibilities shifted from professionals to support staff and from support staff to students. Reassignments and staff reductions resulted in considerable savings in salaries.

Klerk and Euster (1989) also found that there were fewer professionals working in technical services because of the changes to the cataloguing process and at the same time automation is brought about an increased demand on the public service area, where professional librarians now spend more of their time. This is changing the orientation of the library from a warehouse to a client-centered approach. Furuta (1990) stated that the introduction of the bibliographic utilities in the 1970s produced far-reaching changes in cataloging departments by allowing the bulk of the material to be processed more quickly and cost effectively by non-professionals. In turn, that change caused professionals' duties to shift to handling the more difficult items.

Dyer, Fossey and Mckee (1993) stated that technology can have a profound effect on job design and the quality of working life. The introduction of an automated library system brings changes in the working environment, in the nature of the work and job content, in job autonomy and methods of control, in skill requirements, responsibility status and career paths and in patterns of relationships, work groups and communication. Daniels (1995) stated that most of the extra work will be concerned with record conversion, inputting of data and bar-coding the material. The potential that computerized systems have for providing a much improved service has meant that workload has increased in two ways. Firstly, the very effectiveness of them, and the fact that they enable staff to do so much more, has led to the creation of more work. Framework may also arise from tasks such as back up and maintenance - these can sometimes take up more staff time than is originally estimated.

Jones (1999) found that more than half of the total respondents replied that technology increased their workload. The percentages of staff in each library who believed technology has added more responsibilities to their job are even higher 58 percent, 64 percent, and 62 percent. Sykes (1986) discovered that library assistants in one academic library gained satisfaction either from contact with the users or from doing the job efficiently led him to conclude that for those who get their satisfaction from the latter, automation increases job satisfaction. Automation can lead to increased variety, challenge and opportunities for learning and development, especially when the system is being implemented. It can also bring an increased sense of achievement and feeling of usefulness. They assert that job satisfaction is increased in many cases: "mainly by increasing the efficiency and effectiveness with which staff are able to do their jobs".

Daniels (1995) stated that non-professional staff in UK College seemed fairly comfortable with the new system to use for the basic functions. Their increased job satisfaction demonstrated better and more efficient services to the users and enhancement of overall image of library. They were impressed by the way; it had led to improve speed, efficiency, accuracy as well as access to materials. One library stated that it had doubled circulation figures and the other two appreciated the drastic cuts in waiting times.

IMPACT OF INFORMATION TECHNOLOGY (IT) ON LIBRARY USERS

The major reason for using new technology should be that it will ultimately benefit the end user by improving the range and quality of user and support services. One of the major significant challenges facing academic libraries during times of dynamic technology is the ability to understand the changing needs and perspectives of their users. Libraries are more concerned to help users in coping with changing technologies as their potential has significant impact on teaching, education and research activities of academic community,

Pease and Gouke (1982) examined on-line catalog and card catalog use patterns and showed that users preferred online catalogs to card catalogs. Matthews, et al. (1983) surveyed 28 libraries users and non-users of on-line catalogue and reported that after the introduction of the on-line catalog there was an increase in the use of library catalogs and collections. Moreover, users consulted the on-line catalog frequently, found relevant materials in their searches, were satisfied with search results, preferred on-line catalogs to card catalogs, and said on-line catalogs were easy to use without formal instruction. Bichteler (I987) stated that library managers should provide several levels and types of instruction in using the online catalog. Printed material near the terminal may range from a simple flier, which outlines basic operations to a complete manual for more sophisticated users. However, most users prefer online assistance, as they frequently wish to begin searching immediately without taking the time to read instructions or they may be accessing the catalog from a remote location.

Lipetz and Paulson (1987) surveyed users once before and twice after the introduction of an on-line subject catalog to measure its impact on user habits in New York State Library. They found that after the on-line catalog was introduced, the volume of catalog use and the proportion of subject searches were increased. Klobas (1990) stated that users can be useful allies when a new technology is proposed. Indeed, some users push the library to introduce new information technology. Users should therefore be kept informed about new information technology. Informed users should accept and adopt the technology more readily and more quickly than if it was completely new to them. They may even encourage the library or its parent organization to adopt a specific new technology. To keep users informed about technological developments, a 'Technology update' could be made available to them.

Martinez-Arellano (1996) studied user attitudes and behavior before and after implementation of an On-line Catalog in the Central Library of the National Autonomous University of Mexico (UNAM). The study showed that after introducing an on-line catalog in a library, the frequency of library visits was increased the number catalogs users was greater and that opinion about library services was better, use of the catalog was easier, and users found more information on library holdings.

Yacoob and Harun (1996), as the use of IT becomes an increasingly important part of daily life, users have to be educated so that optimum use and advantage of the facilities is ensured. Promoting and encouraging the use of the new library services has been one of the main responsibilities of the library staff. There is an increasing need for user education for novice users. Outreach programmes are needed to market the systems and to teach the formulation of simple and complex Boolean search strategies. Similar instruction is also needed for the use of other applications, such as CDROM, CD-Net and multimedia. Starkweather and Wallin (1999) used two qualitative research methods- focus groups and interviews to explore the experience and concerns of selected faculty of the University of Nevada, Las Vegas. Most participants replied that the library's computer-based information resources affected the way they conducted research. They saved time when searching electronic periodical indexes, they had increased confidence in their review of the literature by using electronic resources, and they could identify resources in remote libraries and archives. It was generally held that online access to catalogs and periodical indexes was very convenient and saved faculty time both by "speeding up" the research process and reducing trips to the library.

Libraries have wide range of opportunities and variety of challenges offered by the rapid development and wide application of Information Technology (IT). It has become an integral part of all library operations and information services. This movement of using IT in libraries has dramatically changed the ways by which data acquisition, processing and access has been carried out and information services have been provided by the libraries. As this technology provides librarians with new choices, new opportunities and new challenges, there has been a phenomenal progress in the use of IT applications in library operations and information services in the developed countries of world. IT usage in Indian libraries has also gained considerable momentum in recent years, which is going to increase at much faster rate in future.

4

Networking of Libraries in India

India has achieved a vast multi-faceted socio-economic development during the last 64 years of its independence. It has made a commendable progress in educational, scientific, technological, engineering, philosophical, social and cultural fields. India has developed during the last 50 years a very large system of education and has created a vast body of men and women equipped with a high order of scientific and technological capabilities, robust humanist and philosophical thought and creativity (Indian National Commission for Cooperation with UNESCO, 1998). Education plays a key role for the development of any society. Library being a treasure house of information, not only gather, store and disseminate information but also serve as an effective agency for creation of fresh ideas and new knowledge. The goal of a library is to provide suitable information materials useful for study, teaching and research purposes in a society. The library functions as conservator of knowledge, ideas, teaching, research, publication, extension and service and interpretation. Libraries supplement the classroom teaching work and provide Wide range of knowledge required to attain intellectual pursuits. A well-equipped library is not only necessary for all teaching and study but also essential for research.

LIBRARIES IN INDIA: PROBLEMS AND CHALLENGES

With the growing importance of management of knowledge resources and providing knowledge-based solutions to various problems, the libraries are supposed to play a pivotal role in the society instead of the peripheral role of assisting in information search and making available the documents having relevant information. Ongoing advancements in ICTs and the growing necessity of managing knowledge resources have influenced almost every facet of libraries and set the process of restructuring, finding new models of planning of these organizations and remodeling of their services keeping in view the new possibilities of meeting users information demands and providing greater conveniences to them. Because of accelerated pace of electronic publishing, digitization of documents, development of library networks and growing emphasis on the internet-based library services, providing just in time access to information on any subject. Quality filtering of enormous volume of information and capturing the high quality information to work processes and information user communities is in fact now a major challenge for society.

In the highly competitive and growing market of electronic information resources, an important area for concern for libraries is, to how to individually or collectively and cost effectively acquire the best of information products and services. As electronic archives are being built and made available online, libraries are doing away with archival role for such information sources and buying online access for them instead of buying the source. On the basis of frequency of use of certain resources, the libraries are also considering paying as per usage instead of acquiring a source of information. A lot of useful information also exists in the open access electronic information resources and academic libraries can collaboratively track, evaluate and pick up sources of common concern and thus create virtual information repositories designed and customized according to their requirements.

Srivastava and Verma (1980), the successful operation and functioning of a library is based on the premise that it should have adequate resources to support training and research, fully trained and qualified staff capable of organising the information contents in the most scientific and helpful order, and the readers who come to use the library and its resources. The most basic requirement for running a academic library is finance. Adequate finance is essential for successful functioning of an academic library. Although, the need for adequate funds for academic libraries has been recommended by various expert committees and commissions, it has not been duly followed and implemented in practice in India. Academic libraries in India have not been provided sufficient funds to acquire information resources to meet the growing information needs of their users. Moreover, library budgets are decreasing every year and cost of documents is increasing day by day. These factors have great impact on the quality and quantity of collection development in academic libraries. Without adequate funds, it is becoming very difficult for academic libraries to provide efficient services to its users.

CHANGING FACE OF INDIAN LIBRARIES

Libraries in India are hybrid libraries and will continue to act as brick and mortar libraries along with click and mortar libraries although the mix between paper and electronic materials will shift somewhat in the passage of time. Majority of the University and college libraries offer internet facilities to their users and some are having their web sites and offering web-based library and information services. The UGC's Information and Library Network (INFLIBNET) provided initial grants and manpower to most Indian university libraries to initiate their automation work.

These libraries are now integrated with the INFLIBNET. Some of them also have connectivity with the Developing Library Network (DELNET). Following the consortia approach, the UGC has also made available the access to a large number of costly e-journals to Indian universities under its UGC-Infonet programme along with necessary hardware such as V-SAT connectivity to these universities.

The Indian academic libraries are in the process of restructuring their facilities and work processes, remodeling their functions and re-engineering their services to facilitate their enhanced role in the new information environment. A number of libraries are digitizing their uniquely held collections. To facilitate compact storage of information, they are even converting their print archives of information to CD-ROMs and DVD-ROMs. Development of databases, application of expert systems, mobile computing and more focused flow of specific information through intranets is likely to have further impact the way services are offered to information user communities. Several Indian networked university libraries have achieved the level of providing any information just at the time of demand. However, they are yet to initiate the next level of much desired service, i.e. just in time delivery of most appropriate and high quality information at the place where desired. On time delivery of any academic information anywhere is important.

In the present information environment, both medium and message are important. User communities are themselves accessing the global information resources and chatting with their colleagues abroad through the Internet medium, university libraries have a challenge to provide worthwhile, qualitative, most engaging, motivating and interesting information which even helps to integrate ideas, links related information and create insights for the generation of new knowledge. In the ever-growing ocean of information hooking and fishing out the worthwhile ideas and information is not a simple task. The challenge for the libraries is to separate relevant qualitative information from trash and make this information available on time to help information user communities to do and accomplish their tasks at hand. As a lot of electronic information is available in unbundled form, repacking of information according to institutional needs and its customization as per users' requirements may become an important activity of the libraries. In the anticipated future, these libraries will not only be under pressure to invent new information products but also be innovating new services which ensure timely access to information according to requirements and conveniences of various categories of users. Maintaining unique and high quality collections, creation and marketing of databases of regional information and indigenous knowledge, constantly adding value and improving quality of services will be critical for Indian academic libraries for their very survival in the internet era.

Indian libraries also face a great challenge of preparing and empowering information user communities by imparting need-based information literacy. For decades, India has not been able to make effective use of its manpower because of illiteracy. India will not be able to make most effective use of its literate manpower without imparting information literacy. The Indian libraries are required to launch massive movement and programmes for imparting information literacy to enhance the capacities and competence of information users to make more effective use of information resources and services.

Library and information personnel play a key role in the development of resources and services of university libraries. Because of fluid information environment and rapidly changing work performance requirements, skill and competency gap is often created in employees. "Any large organization today has to survive, grow and prosper in a highly competitive, dynamic, rapidly changing complex environment, where human obsolescence is as common as that of machines and where survival is only of the fittest" (Bhatia and Singh, 2000). To maintain the competitive level of library professionals, continuing education and need-based training of library staff will be important requirement. Continuing education and training of staff will not only help to enhance their capacity for work performance and ensure efficiency but also help to quickly adopt and properly adapt with new information handling methods, knowledge management tools and technologies and make effective use of contemporary information systems and services. Keeping in view the ever-expanding operations of libraries and new kind of service demands on one hand and limited financial resource on the other, libraries are developing a corporate culture of management. For the university libraries undergoing restructuring, management issues are now as important as technical processes and operations. Libraries are developing their mission statements, objectives and strategies to cut costs and enhance services; they are reorienting their services keeping in view their customers' requirements (Malhan, 2006).

As information technology products and equipment soon become obsolete, the libraries may have to keep provisions for a recurring budget for up gradation of existing and acquisition of new products and equipment. Fund raising, fee-based services, zero-based budgeting, and the most appropriate use of the available financial resources will be very important.

NETWORKING OF LIBRARIES IN INDIA

Accessibility to information has crossed all the geographical boundaries. The access to the library resources has also transformed from "physical access", to "online access". Telecommunications networks form an integral part of accessing, communicating, and transmitting information. In the last two decades, and now in the 21st century, the literature indicates the increase of networks in terms of numbers, geographical area, the variety of devices interconnected, and their application. Library network applications include resource sharing, data sharing, communication, and data exchange. The networking efforts in various countries got a boost with the tremendous and fast developments in computer and communication technologies, which led to the implementation and successful operation of national and international computer-communication networks. These networks were commonly used for business and commercial applications, but the libraries were quick to start efforts to make use of these networks for linking. libraries for resource sharing among them. The success stories of library networks in the advanced countries like the Online Computer Library Center (OCLC), (originally called the Ohio College Library EFFORTS Center when it started in Ohio in 19671, the Washington Library Network (WLN), the Research Library Information Network (RLIN), in the USA, and the British Library Automated Information Service (BLAISE) in UK, etc., are examples of such cases. In India, the Department of Telecommunication (DOT), Videsh Sanchar Nigam Ltd. (VSNL) and the government are responsible for providing and maintaining national and international communication facilities. The existing communication networks in India are as follows (Rao, 2001)

1. INDONET (the first Indian commercial computer communication network)
2. Education and Research Network (ERNET)
3. National Informatics Network (NICNET)
4. Gateway Packet Switching System (GPSS)
5. Remote Area Business Message and Network (RABMAN)
6. National packet switched data network (INET).

INDONET has been in full operation since 1986; the rest of the networks were established between 1986 and 1991. Realizing the need for proper utilization of available resources, several library and information networks have been set up in different parts of India since 1998. These include:

i. Information and Library Network (INFLIBNET)
ii. Bangalore Library Network (BangNet)
iii. Calcutta Library Network (CalibNet)
iv. Delhi Library Network (DelNet)
v. Biotechnology Information System (BTIS)
vi. Madras Library Network (MALIBNET)
vii. Mysore Library network (MYLIBNET)
viii. Scientific and Industrial Research Network (SIRNET)
ix. Pune Library Network (PuneNet).
x. Ahmadabad Library Network (ADINET)

ERNET, which came into existence in 1986 with the assistance of the Government of India and the United Nations Development Programme, involved eight premier institutions in the country as participating agencies. It was the first network in India which provided access to the global Internet, so many institutes like universities made use of its facilities. In 1991, a major national programme initiated by the University Grants Commission gave birth to the formation of INFLIBNET, an autonomous network involved in modernizing university libraries in India and connecting them through a nationwide high speed data network using state-of-the-art technologies for the optimum utilization of information.

1. INFLIBNET (Centre Information and Library Network) is an Autonomous Inter-University Centre (IUC) of University Grants Commission (UGC) involved in creating infrastructure for sharing of library and information resources and services among Academic and Research Institutions. It is a major National Programme initiated by the UGC in March 1991. INFLIBNET works collaboratively with University Libraries in India to shape the future of the academic libraries in the evolving information environment. INFLIBNET is involved in modernizing university libraries in India and connecting them as well as information centres in the country through a nation-wide high speed data network using the state-of-art technologies for the optimum utilisation of information. INFLIBNET is set out to be a major player in promoting scholarly communication among academicians and researchers in India. It promotes automation of libraries, develops standards, creates union catalogue of serials, thesis, books, monographs, and non book materials, provides access to bibliographic information sources, creates database of projects, institutions, specialists. The Centre, on behalf of the UGC, has taken-up a number of new initiatives for the benefit of the academic community. These initiatives include i) Shodhganga: a reservoir of Indian Theses and Dissertations; ii) Shodhgangotri: a repository of approved synopsis submitted to the universities for registration under Ph.D. programme; iii) OJAS@ INFLIBNET: An open access journal publishing platform; iv) Shibboleth-based access management system; v) Open source software R & D; vi) InfoPort: A comprehensive gateway to all Indian electronic scholarly content; vii) e-PG Pathshala: e-Content for PG Courses; and viii) Measuring Research Output of Indian Universities.

2. DELNET (Delhi Library Network) was started at the India International Centre Library in January 1988 and was registered as a society in 1992. It was initially supported by the National Information System for Science and Technology (NISSAT), Department of Scientific and Industrial Research, Government of India. It was subsequently supported by the National Informatics Centre, Department of Information Technology, Ministry of Communications and Information Technology, Government of India and Ministry of Culture, Government of India. DELNET has been established with the prime objective of promoting resource sharing among the libraries through the development of a network of libraries. It aims to collect, store, and disseminate information besides offering computerised services to users, to coordinate efforts for suitable collection development and also to reduce unnecessary duplication wherever possible. DELNET gives membership to various libraries including universities, colleges, government departments and provides technical assistance to them for creating and maintaining the bibliographic databases, serials control, union catalogue preparations, abstracting services, inter library loan, document transfer/ copying facilities and for accessing local, national and international databases. It has also created library software such as DELSEARCH, DEL-DOS etc for library networking database creation and database access using different platforms.

3. **ADINET** is a network of libraries in and around Ahmadabad. It was registered as a Society in October 1994. It was initially sponsored by National Information System for Science and Technology (NISSAT), Department of Scientific and Industrial Research, Government of India. ADINET aims to bring about cooperative mode of working amongst the libraries and information centers in and around Ahmadabad. The main objective of ADINET is to promote sharing of resources and disseminate information among member libraries by networking them and creating a centralized Union catalogue of their holdings. It plans to coordinate efforts for suitable collection development and reduce unnecessary duplication wherever possible. ADINET will not only help library users but will be of help to individuals who practice different professions in getting specialized information of their interest.131 A centralized database of periodicals and databases available in libraries of Ahmadabad is being created by ADINET. Records collected from participating libraries are being suitably formatted and merged to generate Union Catalogue of Ahmadabad libraries. With cooperation of participating libraries, these databases are being regularly updated. At present this database includes only the present/ current holdings of libraries.

4. **CALIBNET** (Calcutta Library Network) has been launched by National Information System for Science and Technology, Department of Science and Industrial Research in the city of Calcutta. It is launching its library network programs, facilitating remote online access to the holding

data of Calcutta libraries, and other specialized databases as well — a significant step towards bibliographic resources sharing amongst Calcutta libraries. It is also providing electronic access to globally available information, imbibing its 'information centre approach'. Both are essential for advanced learning and scholarship. In the process, CALIBNET aims at covering a wide panorama of information end-user interests, with diffusion of new electronic information technology as the primary concern.

5. MYLIBNET (Mysore Library network) was established at Mysore city in the year 1995 and the Central Food Technological Research Institute (CFTRI), Mysore, being an active member of Mysore City Library Consortium (MCLC), is hosting this network in its premises. MYLIBNET is working closely with MCLC to promote information services in Mysore city.

MYLIBNET is also having the same objectives like other library networks in India but with a difference. One of the main objectives of this network is to prepare a union catalogue of periodicals subscribed by the member libraries. Accordingly, most of the library networks have been compiling the catalogue either in hard copy or in electronic form. Due to information technology advancement, this catalogue is now made available on the Internet.

MYLIBNET has also compiled this catalogue in the year 1996 in the machine-readable form and developed a software package (floppy disk version) for searching this catalogue either by institution name, journal title or by keywords. This software was released to its members in July 1996.

In order to have faster communication among libraries, MYLIBNET has been subscribing to electronic mail service of Education and Research Network (ERNET) of Department of Electronics (DoE), Govt. of India. Since the mail hub was located at Bangalore, which is 140 km away from Mysore city, all the members were provided with telephones with

STD facility by their parent institutions to access e-mail service. Library and information science professionals from member institutions were trained on e-mail operation. Now MYLIBNET is bringing reality to its networking activity by providing Web-enabled facility to its member libraries to modify the union catalogue database online.

6. Scientific and Industrial Research Network (SIRNET) is proposed to interconnect all the CSIR laboratories and other R & D institutions of India. The main objective of SIRNET is to harness the vast S & T information sources available with national laboratories and inculcate the habit of resource sharing among them. The ultimate aim of SIRNET is to link entire scientific community of nation with the national library system and the international links to achieve efficient scientific communication.

In the first phase Electronic Mail has been implemented bringing high pitch response from all CSIR laboratories. The other R & D institutions of the country are also coming upon network.

The transfer of file from one machine to another is an integral part of a computer network. The file may be an ASCII file, binary file, or a text file. Presently, only ASII can be transferred by UUCP protocol and the SIRNET protocol will enable both the ASCII and binary files to be transferred in due course.

Computer communication technology would be utilized for document transfer. The fascimile transmission, used presently, is not recommended on network because of heavy expenditure involved in it.

To support R & D activities at the national level NISCAIR is designing and developing databases in various disciplines of science. Following databases at present available online through direct dial up mode:

- National Union Catalogue of Scientific Serials in India.
- Current Contents of Indian Journals (ISCOMM).
- Polymer science database.

- Material science bibliographic database.
- Catalogue of scientific and technical conference proceedings.

7. Pune Library Network (PuneNet) is a joint programme of the University of Pune, the Centre for Development of Advanced Computing (C-DAC) and the National Chemical Laboratory (NCL) being funded by National Information System for Science and Technology (NISSAT) of the Department of Scientific and Industrial Research (DSIR), Government of India. It is hosted in the Bioinformatics Centre. It maintains centralized databases of information resources available in the participating libraries.

The main objectives of Pune-Net are:

- To interconnect all the libraries in the Pune city through a computer communication network.
- To facilitate active information exchange, and enable users to keep themselves up-to-date as to the availability of books and journals at various libraries of Pune city.
- To help in increasing cooperation amongst the participating libraries and coordinate the activities so as to serve the user community efficiently, and
- To provide various information services to all participant libraries and their users by using various information sources, CD-ROMs and Web-based databases.

At present Pune-Net hosts the databases mentioned below. These databases are updated yearly. Users can search these databases online using its Web site.

Database of Books : The database contains 1,08,853 records from 20 participant libraries of Pune-Net. A user can conduct simple or Boolean searches to locate his desired item.

Union Catalogue of Periodicals : This database

contains 6425 records pertaining to various libraries in the Pune city. Currently data from 60 libraries are available online.

Booksellers database : There are several booksellers in Pune . Pune-Net is trying to provide information on the books available with these booksellers. This will be of great help to librarians and users to locate latest books in subjects of their interest. Currently, Pune-Net has two bookseller's data on its server and more data from other booksellers will be added in near future. The booksellers are keen in sharing this information with Pune-Net.

LIS professionals database : A database of LIS professionals has been created using Microsoft Access. This database provides information about library professionals working in Pune City with their subject expertise.

Pune-Net libraries database : A database of libraries participating in Pune-Net has been created using Microsoft Access. From this database users can find details of each library, viz. name, research area, name of the librarian, rules, timings, etc. The database is updated regularly.

Direct access to libraries : Access to C-DAC and Jayakar Library has been provided on-line through HTML interface. This has become possible because of the existing University Fibre Optic Network. Using this facility the user can directly access these libraries, and get more information regarding the lending status of a particular book (issued, on shelf, etc.) It gives not only access to the books recorded in these databases of these libraries but also the holdings of the libraries including CD-ROM databases, microfiche, video cassettes, etc. With the commissioning of the link between NCL and Bioinformatics Centre, NCL library data has become accessible directly from Pune-Net.

Data Standardization

Data from participating libraries is being collected and stored at the Pune-Net server. Each participating library is using different library management software. Standardized data input becomes vital under such circumstances. Pune-Net is following its own standard, based on the international standard for information exchange - ISO 2709. This also helps in indexing.

Pune-Net Services

Apart from Pune-Net database services, it provides also the following services to users.

1. E-mail and Internet Connectivity : Pune-Net not only provides e-mail facility to participating libraries but also acts as a gateway to the Internet. In all, 36 libraries are using e-mail and Internet facilities. Because of the installation of three telephone lines, users are able to access the Pune-Net server and data several times without any difficulty.

2. CD-ROM Database Services : Pune-Net subscribes to a few bibliographic databases on CD-ROM, such as Inside Science Plus and Inside Humanities and Social Sciences by BLDSC. It provides table of contents (TOC) service based on over 10,000 high impact current serials.

LIBRARY CONSORTIA IN INDIA

With the proliferation of library automation and with library users having more sophisticated computer skills, no single library is well enough equipped to accommodate its own users. Cooperation among libraries has become more important and has encouraged the significant growth of consortia, which assist libraries in joint purchasing, interlibrary loan, database sharing for cataloging, and the use of the same automation system. The library consortia are association of libraries established by formal agreement, usually for the purpose of improving services through resource sharing among its members. Resource sharing is basically sharing of resources of participating libraries on the basis of the agreement of cooperation for the purpose of sharing the resources of each other's materials. This entails not only to share the document resources but also facilitates services, equipments and even the manpower among the participating libraries. The Libraries have started using the computers in large number and have automated their functions and services. After the introduction of internet in Libraries, the concept of on-line resources was introduced and the libraries started subscribing e-journals regularly. The traditional sources of information i.e. books, journals, magazines are supplemented by electronic forms of documents e-books, e-journals, e- newspaper etc. The automated libraries get connected to one or the other networks. A computer network allows the user of one computer to use the resources of another computer which may be space, database, programs or printer. The traditional libraries were facing barriers for interlibrary loan such as indifferences of lending library, conservative attitude, distance, language, cost time etc. The recent developments in Information science, Computer and Telecommunication technologies have changed these perceptions on account of multidimensional growth of published documents. The modern libraries with the advanced technology are forming library consortium for sharing electronic resources. The purpose of library network is to promote resource sharing among member libraries by coordinate efforts for suitable collection development and reduce the unnecessary duplication wherever possible. The purpose of the library network is to provide network based services to Users, document Delivery Services, bibliographic Information Services, and human Resource Development. Activities and functions undertaken by a library consortium may vary to a great extent, but often compromise of cooperative collection development, education and training, preservation, centralised services and network alliances featuring library automation services, system support, inter-library lending, union listing, retrospective conversion, consultation and cooperative purchasing.

i. Cooperative purchasing of E-resources is one of the

key activities of a library consortium. The concept of consortium itself has evolved from the idea of cooperation, coordination and collaboration. Collaborative arrangements for acquisition and management of electronic information resources can result in lower prices and saving in terms of actual cost, time and staff. Moreover, access to resources is now considered more important than collection building itself especially if the access is perpetual in nature.

ii. The consortium facilitates the libraries to get the benefit of wider access to electronic resources at affordable cost and on the best terms of licenses. A consortium, with the collective strength of resources of various institutions available to it, is in a better position to address and resolve the problems of managing, organising and archiving the electronic resources. Moreover, the technology has changed expectations of researchers, their patience, and their willingness to accept services that are available on demand. Moreover, accessibility-to full-text resources and online bibliographic databases to the students, researchers and faculty improves their research productivity in terms of number of research publications given the fact that there exists a very high degree of correlation between the scientific literature available to researchers in a given organization and scientific productivity of researchers and research organization in terms of number of research articles produced. The consortium, as a platform for member libraries not only facilitates sharing of print and electronic resources, it also works as a catalyst to trigger other activities that require collaborative efforts, such as union catalogue of books, joint automation projects, etc.

In a country like India where the Government of India is funding three-quarters of education and research, national consortium is the most practical solution. A national consortium can greatly reduce duplication of efforts and provide greater purchasing power. A national consortium would be in a better position to handle archival issues. Federating the activities of all the consortia initiatives through a common forum can lead to a national consortium for a certain category of E-journal purchase, and more particularly for sharing the infrastructure and service costs and facilities. Developing country-archive infrastructure is an area that fits the role of a national consortium well (Arora, 2003). There have been a few national and regional efforts to provide shared WWW-based electronic resources amongst scientific and technical libraries in India. The following are some of the major efforts.

1. Indian National Digital Library in Engineering Science & Technology (INDEST) : The Ministry of Human Resource Development (MHRD) has set-up the "Indian National Digital Library in Engineering Sciences and Technology (INDEST) Consortium" The Ministry provides funds required for subscription to electronic resources for 48 institutions including, like IIS, IIT, NIT, IIM and a few other centrally funded Government institutions through the consortium headquarters set-up at the IIT, Delhi. Besides, many Government or Government-aided engineering colleges and technical universities have joined the Consortium with financial support from the AICTE. Moreover, the INDEST-AICTE Consortium, as an open-ended proposition, welcomes other institutions to join it on their own for sharing benefits it offers in terms of highly discounted rates of subscription and better terms of agreement with the publishers. All electronic resources being subscribed are available from the publisher's Website. The Consortium has an active mailing list and a Web site hosted at the IIT, Delhi. The Consortium is the most ambitious initiative taken so far in the country. The benefit of consortia-based subscription to electronic resources is not confined to major technological institutions in the country but is also extended to all AICTE-accredited and UGC-affiliated institutions. It is a consortium of engineering and technological libraries for nurturing a core of digital collections in engineering and technology. It is proposed as a central national resource of full-text digital information in engineering and technology. The contributions from participating institutions are proposed to be diverted directly from funding agencies to the INDEST. The INDEST is hosting a variety of Web-based digital resources, including those available through national and international agencies with consortia and national licenses, to provide access to authorized users in India. 1096 engineering colleges and institutions have already joined the consortium on their own. Recently 198 engineering colleges and institutions joined under self-support- new scheme.

2. UGC-Infonet E-Journals Consortium : Universities in India are facing challenges due to budget cuts, reduced staff, devaluation of Indian rupee against major currencies and the escalation in the cost of foreign publications. Due to these factors, there has been a continuous reduction in the subscription to scholarly journals and databases, which greatly affects research and academic activity. Realizing the need for a common mechanism for access to scholarly information, the Chairman of UGC set the priority to provide access to scholarly information for the research and academic community by supplementing the existing collection in the individual universities. The professional periodical literature is now available over the Internet to the University community through UGC-Infonet E-Journals Consortium. This will provide a great boost to the research and development work in the universities across the country. UGC-Infonet E-Journals Consortium has facilitated free access to scholarly journals and databases in all areas of learning to the research and academic community. This initiative helped to get a discount of more than 85% –90% on many scholarly journals and databases and enables the research and academic community to have greater access to resources.

i. Agreement of Co-operation amongst IITs, BARC and TIFR (1998): The idea for a consortium of IITs in India was first mooted in 1995 for subscriptions to printed journals in 1995 in the annual meeting of IIT Librarians at IIT, Bombay. The librarians of Bhabha Atomic Research Centre (BARC), Trombay and the Tata Institute of Fundamental Research (TIFR), Bombay also participated in the meeting. Although rationalization of periodical subscriptions in the printed format had limited impact, it did trigger a highly active resource sharing programmes amongst IITs, BARC, and TIFR in India. However, in subsequent annual meetings of the IIT, the librarians' decisions for consortia-based subscriptions of electronic journals were made and an "Agreement of Cooperation" was signed accordingly.

ii. The consortia of libraries of IITs, BARC, and TIFR tried working out consortia-based subscriptions to electronic journals through a number of publishers including Elsevier Science (Science Direct), John Wiley (Wiley Interscience), Springer-Verlag (Link Information Services), and Academic Press (Project Ideal) for the year 2000, but without much success. Initiatives are being taken for the consortia-based subscriptions for the year 2001.

3. STI Network for resource sharing amongst Science and Technology Libraries (1999) : The proposal for the formation of "STI Network" was initiated at a meeting of the heads of major science and technology libraries held at the Defense Scientific Information and Documentation Centre (DESIDOC) in May 1999. The STI Network has 20 major libraries in India as signatories to its Memorandum of Understanding (MoU) with a provision to induct additional members. The resources sharing in all modes and subscriptions to electronic resources as a consortium of libraries are the major objectives of the STI networks. The STI Network is an initiative which now lies dormant.

4. The IIM (Indian Institutes of Management) Consortium : All IIMs developed a consortium to subscribe e-journals centrally. The objective was to ensure among the IIMs, optimum utilization and enhancement of the resources, and to minimize the expenditure by consortia based subscriptions to the commonly subscribed databases and journals. The idea was to approach publishers of Electronic journals and CD-ROM Databases to begin with, as a consortium for better pricing and services. A pilot study conducted during 1999 revealed that more than 60% of IIM s electronic resources were overlapping. The additional burden while accessing all the electronic titles across the IIMs for the individual print subscriptions at each of the institutes was shared equally by working out the license charges for the Enhanced Access License(EAL). Over 1050 E-journals are directly sourced from publishers and over 12500 E-journals aggregated full text the IIMs are able to get online access across all the institutes by paying a nominal additional amount.

5. FORSA Consortia : FORSA stands for Forum for Resource Sharing in Astronomy and Astrophysics, which was established in 1982, for sharing the resources in astronomy libraries in the country. In 2004, this group has extended its membership to Physics and Mathematics libraries in the country who have common interests. Currently FORSA has twelve members. FORSA member libraries have automated their collection, give access to electronic journals, Inter-Library Loan for resource sharing among the member libraries, and provide document delivery services either by speed post, fax or telephone.

6. CSIR (Council of Scientific and Industrial Research) Consortium : CSIR has also formed a consortium for which National Institute of Science, Communication and Information Resources (NISCSIR), a constituent establishment of CSIR formed with the merger of INSDOC and NISCOM, has been identified as nodal agency. To augment CSIR research and development activities, NISCAIR implemented an agency for the process of providing access to globally available electronic journals to the entire S & T staff of CSIR. On behalf of CSIR, it has entered into an agreement with Elsevier science to access its odd 1,500 e-journals and intends to strengthen further its information resources base by subscribing access to more journals published globally. CSIR consortium extended its access by creating appropriate on consortium basis with the other providers of e-journals.

7. J-GATE from Informatics India : The J-GATE interface, launched recently by Informatics India, proposes to serve as an electronic aggregator, third-party gateway, and electronic archival facility for several thousand scientific journals. J-GATE, like Cross reference proposes to host a large database consisting of bibliographic references and abstracts of journal articles, with links to their full-text articles at the publisher's site. J-GATE would provide Web-based access to the full text of journals to the libraries, wherever applicable, if their print versions are subscribed to through them. Users' authentication will be done by the J-GATE interface. J-GATE also facilitates and initiates the formation of library consortia by pooling journal subscribers from a given publisher.

5

Trends of Information Technology in Libraries

Information Technology has gone under several changes since its inception, particularly in electronic and digital era. Staring from the formation of clay tablets in Babylonian civilization, it has traveled for its evolution through paper age, punched cards up to electronics media, particularly the computer. The application of technology in libraries has been a subject of interest to professional librarians. More recently libraries have sought to implement increasingly complex solutions that involve distributed networking and access to remote information resources. The important features that have affected the quality of information are accuracy, comprehensiveness, freshness and time. The information technology can be used in the libraries to support technical functions associated with technical processing and circulation work, to support information storage, retrieval and dissemination systems, to support management of information services in libraries and for extension services. Since 1960s worldwide libraries have been using technology in general and computers in particular to automate a wide range of administrative, technical tasks and information services. During last two decades, information technology has played an increasingly influential role in library management system and services.

Cortez (1983) defined a management information system as ' an automated library system with design features to help in the performance of management decision-making. It has dual function to support day-to-day library operations as well as to provide management with useful information for decision making'. Bichteler (1987) stated that automated system allow more objective, quantitative and monitoring of work. Rowley (1993) stated that most of the library management systems offer an extensive set of standard reports relating to transactions in various functions in the system. In electronic era, the information technology has different fields that have impact on the life of human being as well as the information management. The technologies are being utilized for the library activities such as digital products, internet, multimedia and networking. Badu (1993) surveyed staff and students to study the impact of the use of microcomputers on the University of Ghana library. He found that 50% of the library staff were very excited and felt it would improve services, gained library a better corporate image and some satisfaction to staff. Respondents stated that borrowing transaction through computer is completed rapidly compared with manual transactions, which took minutes instead of seconds. Sharma's (1993) study conducted on the use of computer in libraries of higher education showed that the time taken in processing 500 books in a library manually as well as through computer was 1000 hours and 60 hours respectively. The point to be noted that the time required for typing/data entry was the same number of 40 hours for both the systems. This shows that a computerised system is about 50 times cost-effective compared to non-computerised one for the university libraries. Ganpule and Waydande (1994) stated that library automation brought efficiency in house-keeping jobs in IIT Library Bombay. It helped to bring the list of additions weekly instead of fortnightly with improved quality. Hauptman and Anderson (1994) surveyed 800 different types of American libraries and found that technology results in an improved perception of our role, statue and upgraded our image among patrons. Reported that libraries lack enough money and staff training and staff felt technological innovations put more pressure and are stressful. Wright (1995) stated that in automated integrated online library systems, a wide range of reports can be generated from the systems about every part of library activities. The availability of appropriate statistics and summary report related to a particular library function makes planning, evaluation and justification of the library's service much easier. Computer based system can provide a variety of complex information in all library operations for many library management decisions. Himmelfarb (1999) stated that we are experiencing a revolution, not only in library services but in the very conception of the library. Now with the electronic revolutions it is not only the library catalogue is computerised but the computer can call up a variety of other catalogues, indexes, databases, CD-ROMs, Internet as well as books, journals, newspapers, archives, even manuscript collections from other libraries. Potentially, at least, the electronic revolution makes even smaller libraries the equivalent of libraries in major research universities and scholarly institutions.

In today's library environment of decreasing budgets and increasing accountability and demands, library managers are called upon to monitor the functioning of the library regularly to assess the efficiency of library operations in order to make decisions about changes in the way, library functions. A computerised library system provides comprehensive, reliable, relevant, up-to-date and specific information useful to the management quickly on various library activities required by the management for taking effective decisions. Library and information systems developers created the technologic landscape; several separate applications were established to support end user access to information. Some of these developments were about content, and some focused on dissemination. All support increased end user access to digitally recorded document surrogates or primary knowledge records. To date these developments have included: Integrated Library Systems, Online, Databases, Web-Based Resources, Digital Library Collections, e-Books and e-Journals. Typical integrated library systems include functionality in support of acquisitions, cataloging, circulation control, materials booking, serials control, and online catalogs. Initially developed as standalone solutions to a library's processing and service's needs, these applications are now increasingly "welded at the seams" with other services, such as access to online databases. The online database industry began as a separate marketplace in the early 1970s. Now is closely coupled with integrated library systems solutions to provide end users a "one-stop" desktop access point for materials held both locally and licensed internationally. World Wide Web has allowed database producers a clear route for disseminating their resources to a wider audience in many instances directly to the end user.

Web-based resources moved to the forefront in the mid-1990s after libraries determined that users had begun to spend much of their time browsing the web searching for relevant materials that could be conveniently delivered to their desktop in digital fashion. Professional librarians began to think like users in terms of "one-stop shopping" for information and. having been successful at grafting their online catalogs with electronic database resources they next turned their attention to the numerous resources available on the web using their expertise to identify, validate and organize information content they sought to build "portals" that offered access not only to information that was held or licensed by the library but also to information readily available on the Web. Libraries are continuing to develop new Web portals as new resources are created and made accessible via the Internet.

The Digital Library movement has begun to evolve from its early research platform to more fully developed applications typically in selected content areas. As funding sources continue to be identified, we are now seeing the development of specialized collections in digital format aimed squarely at end users. The concept of the digital library is rather encompassing and currently we are seeing only the first efforts at creating environments for storing and disseminating digital content. The notion of eBooks includes both e-Journals and e-Texts. In March 2000 Stephen King released a 66-page novella. Riding the Bullet, as an eBook exclusively for publication via the Web, a half million copies sold in the first 24 hours. Scholarly publishers already compete for the click of the end users' mouse and both online full-text databases and e-Journals are examples of their positioning and strategy. The day will come one would likely see more developments as creative minds begin to design new services and then market them directly to the end user via the networked desktop.

The benefits of using IT in libraries may be consolidated as: improved efficiency of library operations, Improved quality of existing services, Introduced new services, Improved Collection Management, Improved accuracy and control, Increased ability to share resources, Improved image, Improved management information, Eliminate duplication of efforts, Rapid communication, Perform tasks not possible by the manual system, Improved uniformity and standardisation, Improved user satisfaction, Facilitate effective utilisation of funds and Facilitate to market library services.

GLOBAL SCENARIO

The new technologies in libraries Sun Micro Systems (2003) points that the traditional ILS capabilities have been improved, at the same time entirely new technology tools have been created in response to the growth of electronic library resources. Digitization and digital media management (DMM), expanded OPAC, virtual reference/ reference linking and personalized portals are some of the enhancements of technology. Frey (2005) traced ten key trends that are affecting the development of the next generation library. He also mentions that these are not the only trends, but ones that have been selected to give clear insight into the rapidly changing technologies and equally fast changing mindset of library patrons. Communication systems are continually changing the way people access information;

All technology ends. All technologies commonly used today will be replaced by something new;

i. Reached the ultimate small particle for storage
ii. Search Technology will become increasingly more complicated
iii. Time compression is changing the lifestyle of library patrons
iv. Over time we will be transitioning to a verbal society
v. The demand for global information is growing exponentially
vi. The Stage is being set for a new era of Global Systems

The technology has transitioning from a product-based economy to an experience based economy Libraries will transit from a centre of information to a centre of culture: It will not only serve as an information resource, but much more with the exact mission and goals evolving and changing over time.

Breeding (2005) forecasted the trends: the Integrated Library System (ILS) will be reintegrated; the business landscape will change; Players in Broader industries will become involved; Libraries will consolidate automation efforts and the products and services from commercial vendors will continue to dominate. Morgan (2006) traced features like web-blogs, social networking, open source s/w, meta-search standards, mass digitisation, digital resource management (DRM), licensed content growing discontent with library catalogue and OCLC expansion as top technology trends for ALA. In the year 2006 American Library Association identified that the need to engage library community with Google and commercial service providers, the challenge of succession plan, challenge of communication library stories to outsiders, need for continuing education and training for library workers, tailoring library services to respond to user needs, increasing salaries and benefits of librarians as the issues facing the library community. Mfrisque (2006) identifies Basic IT skills for staff, knowledge of hard ware and software and trouble shooting, online help desk, ability to move/talk with customers, empowering staff, creating technical team, educating staff and users on use of technology and e-resources as some of the core competencies to be addressed by that the library professionals.

INDIAN SCENARIO

Libraries play a pivotal role in ensuring the success of higher degrees of research. The important activities of university libraries include collection development, reference services, document delivery, user education, access to resources held by the library, access to other library resources, and access to electronic resources. With the development of Information and Communication Technologies (ICT), university libraries are expected to provide cost effective and reliable access to information using state-of-the art information technology tools. The developments in the Information Technology sector have overcome distance and time. University libraries are fertile areas for the introduction of ICT to make accessible the best possible information from anywhere any time and from any sources. Networks are essential partners in this exercise as they facilitate easy access to vast information services. Networks have the potential to improve library services in several ways.

The continuous improvement in networking technology helps libraries reduce the cost of information provision, thus creating new opportunities for libraries to play a role in information provision for their end users. Library and Information Centers are increasingly being called upon to provide more relevant, up-to-date and timely information to a wide range of users at an affordable cost. The libraries in India, like those in most developing countries, suffer from inadequate funding or stringent budget cuts. This has affected the level of services offered to users both in terms of quality of collections and the degree of staff support provided. In the present circumstances, only a few libraries can afford to have a wide range of information resources within their budget. This had led to the practice of resource sharing, by using cooperative purchases through consortia. INFLIBNET (Information and Library Network) Centre has taken a number of initiatives over the last 10 years, including the recent initiative of UGC-Infonet E-Journals Consortium, to support the Research and Academic community working in these universities.

Over the years, Indian universities have used ICT to provide effective information services. The results of this study show that university libraries in India are at various stages of development in the application of ICT to their day-to-day activities. Virtually all academic libraries depend on the ICT systems for basic operations such as acquisitions, cataloguing, circulation, and serials control. The vast information sources the library gives access to are not only the items held by or owned by the library, but also include remote information sources. Providing access to remote sources is the key challenge for the modern academic librarian (Arrant and Payne, 2001).

Digital Libraries in India

With the advent of digital technology and Internet connectivity, the library scenario is changing fast. Digital technology, Internet connectivity and physical content can be dovetailed resulting in Digital Library. Data available in physical form has been preserved digitally in Digital Library. Digital Libraries have the ability to enhance access to information and knowledge. Recent developments in information and communication technology (ICT), especially the Internet and the Web, have brought significant changes in the ways the information being generated, distributed, accessed, and being used (Bansode and Pujare, 2008).

The explosion of digital information has caught us unprepared to handle the threats posed by rapidly changing technologies and digital obsolescence of computer hardware, software, file formats and storage media. The possibilities of data corruption, physical damage and disasters continue to endanger digitally encoded information. The obsolescence of digital content, e-records and the evidentiary proofs can create problems in administrative, judiciary and legislative functions in addition to loss of valuable information, intellectual property and heritage for future generations. Our digital universe includes text, images, documents, e-files, audio, video, 3D models, web pages, maps, datasets, big data, computer generated microfiche and various other forms of digital information across variety of domains. Therefore, it is necessary to ensure that the digital content and e-records in all forms of human heritage have to be preserved for access and use in future. It is challenging to ensure the discoverability, accessibility, usability, reliability and authenticity of such digital information over a long period. Therefore, it is necessary to develop Trusted Digital Repositories supported by tools, technologies, standards, best practices and policy for long-term preservation and access.

1. The mission is to create a portal for the Digital Library of India which will foster creativity and free access to all human knowledge. It is piloted by the Ministry of Communication and Information Technology, India in coordination with Indian Institute of Science, Bangalore and in collaboration with Carnegie Melon University, USA. Under the collaborative management, scanners for these centres were provided by Carnegie Melon University, USA, under its Million Book Universal Digital Library Programme. Eleven

academic institutions, six religious and cultural institutions, four government and research agencies, and two research institutions in India are participating in this programme.

2. INFLIBNET (www.dspace.inflibnet.ac.in) INFLIBNET has developed a digital library by using Dspace, an open source software. So far INFIBNET has digitised their conference proceeding namely, Caliber and Planner. INFLIBNET provide users the facility to download the full-text articles from its databases..
3. Kalasampada (http://www.ignca.gov. in/dgt_0001.htm) Recognising the need to encompass and preserve the distributed fragments of Indian art and culture, and to serve as a major resource centre for the arts, the Indira Gandhi National Centre for the Arts (IGNCA) in collaboration with Ministry of Communication and Information Technology, initiated a project, Kalasampda (digital library: resources of Indian cultural heritage), for the development of databank of cultural heritage. Kalasampada provides access to over couple of lakhs of manuscripts, over a lakhs of slides, thousands of rare books, rare photographs, audio, and video along with highly researched publications of the IGNCA from a single window.
4. Librarians Digital Library (https:// drtc.isibang.ac.in/) this library has been developed by Documentation Research & Training Centre (DRTC), and contains full-text of papers/articles related to Indian librarianship. Presently, it contains full-text papers submitted in DRTC seminars, papers submitted by LIS professionals, and theses/dissertations of students. It also has plans to include conference proceedings of Indian LIS Associations.
5. Nalanda Digital Library (http://www. nalanda.nitc.ac. in/) Nalanda Digital Library initiated in 1999 at the

National Institute of Technology (NIT), Calicut, is one of the largest digital libraries in the country. Nalanda helps members of the NIT in meeting their academic and research needs by providing timely and up-to-date information with value added services in all the areas of science, engineering, and technology.

6. National Library of India (www.nlindia.org) The library preserves the scanning and archives the rare and brittle books and other documents on compact disc. The library will digitise the books and documents published before 1900 and available Indian publications prior to 1920. So far, 6,600 selected books in Indian and English languages have already been scanned and stored.
7. Raman Research Institute (http:// dspace.rri.res.in/) Raman Research Institute has digitised the research publications of the faculty, students, and the publication of the institute. The Institute has also digitised its annual reports and newspaper clippings.
8. Universal Digital Library (http:// www.iiita.ac.in/ research/udl.html) Universal Digital Library seeks to digitise books of common interest to different communities of interest (COI) and make them available in a manner that is independent of language, location, and time. A complete solution for this was developed by Carnegie-Mellon University, USA involving state-of-the-art planetary scanners for scanning, cropping, OCR, and XML converting. Apart from Indian Institute of Science (IISc), other Indian institutions involved in this project are NCST Mumbai, and IIIT, Hyderabad.
9. Vidyanidhi Digital Library and e-scholarship Portal (http://210.212. 200.226/index.html) Vidyanidhi is an information infrastructure, a digital library, a portal of resources and tools, and facilities doctoral research in India. Vidyanidhi is envisioned to evolve as a national repository and a consortium for e-theses

through participation and partnership with universities, academic institutions, and other stake holders. It will enhance the access to Indian theses and will also enlarge the reach and audience for Indian doctoral research works.

10. Development of ETD, many research and academic institutions have taken initiative to develop Electronic Theses and Dissertation (ETD) library in India. ETD basically includes theses and dissertations submitted in their own institution. Some of the prominent among these institutions are: IISc, Bangalore (http://etd.ncsi.iisc.ernet.in/); IIT Delhi, New Delhi (http://eprint.iitd.ac.in/ dspace/); Indira Gandhi Institute of Development Research, Mumbai (http://oii.igidr.ac.in:8888/dspace/)

Digital library initiatives in India are still in a nascent stage of development. The digital environment in the Indian context is a new concept. Libraries, which would like to develop a digital library, must make careful planning and undertake feasibility study, as digital library projects requires careful selection of hardware, software, materials and standards to be used in their preservation. The sustainability of digital libraries is difficult unless organisations have good budgetary support and quality manpower.

Web Technology & Services

Web-based information systems use a client-server architecture in which the server sends HTML markup to the user's browser, which then renders this HTML and displays it to the user. Along with HTML markup, a server may send JavaScript code that executes in the user's browser. This JavaScript code can in turn contact the original server or additional servers and include information obtained from them into the rendered content while it is being displayed. This basic architecture allows for myriad possible design choices and combinations for mash-ups. Each design choice has implications to ease of use, customizability, programming requirements, hosting requirements, scalability, latency, and availability. The growth of World Wide Web also known as www, or simply the web has been one of the most remarkable development in the history of documentation. Web is popularly used as the synonymous term of World Wide Web or Internet or online. The web is client or server system used to access all kinds of information to anyone on the net. The information can be in the form of regular text, hypertext, pictures, sounds, use net news groups and other types of data. To access information from web, use client program called browser is necessary. In the web, information are stored in pages and each page can hold not only information but links to other pages. In each page a particular word or sequences of words are highlighted and there is a link between the highlighted item and other information, this is called hypertext.

Web services are the latest technology for enabling distributed computing. Web service provides a way to describe their interfaces with enough detail as to allow a user to build a client application to access their functionality. A web service is a software system designed to support computer to computer interaction over the internet. Web services go beyond the functionality of simple web pages and provide dynamic application functionality that can be remotely invoked. Library services refer to facilities that are provided by a library for the use of books and dissemination of information and meet the user's requirement. The well-known existing library services are cataloguing, classification, circulation services, reservation renewal, new arrivals, current contents, current awareness services, selective dissemination of information, indexing and abstracting, reference service, document delivery , interlibrary loan, externally purchased databases, access to other library catalogues, access to online databases, internally published newsletter, reports and journals, bibliographic services and so on. With the increasing use of

Internet all these services has now changed its mode to web environment. Email is widely used by publishers and researchers. TOCs and RSS feeds are being circulated by using email service. Email is a web based excellent medial and most probably the most popular media. Library can use this web medium for various purposes specially for delivering some web based services.

LIBRARY WEBPAGE

Library webpage is very much essential for any library. It is a useful tool to keep informed about library activities and new services. It saves the time of the user, which is more important. The online, web based journals opens rich and variegated new vistas. Clearly, library webpage allow easy bridging of distances. The internet leaps over continents. All libraries whose aim is to support research in concerned subject must maintain library webpage. Libraries may put services provided by them on web to serve user community such as Library collection; Library timing/working days; Library rules; Library services CAS/SDI/Reference services; New books; Recent issues of journals; List of subscribed online journals; Software list; Latest issues of journals; Popular Documents - based on circulation and reservations; Place reservation / hold on certain documents; Outstanding List - renewal facility optional; Procurement request for purchasing new books and other media; Approve document for procurement; User feedback.

Now a day many libraries use chatting system to interact with its users. Web based chat requires different software and more sophisticated set up. In web based chat system enquirers go to a specific page on the library site and connect with the librarian to seek an answer to their information requirements. The software allows the librarian to push pages to an enquirer co-browse where both are able to view the same page and save the chat session if necessary. A Blog is a website, usually maintained by an individual, with regular entries of commentary, descriptions of events, or other material such as graphics or video (Wikipedia, 2009). Blogs provide control to an individual or group of individuals for publishing contents or making commentary on it. Technologically, blogs are easier to use platform-independent and accessible online over the internet. Blogs are increasingly used by libraries as promotional alerting and marketing tools, providing a useful method of promoting new services, alerting users to changes and offering advice and support. In library blogs typical posting include information about fresh arrivals, e-databases, news and services rendered can be flashed for wider effects.

Instant Messaging Services is one of the real-time electronic consulting and reference offered by academic libraries via specific software running on the Internet platform. It is virtually instantaneous communication between two or more people using textual format, providing "real time reference "services, where patrons can synchronously communicate with librarians much as they would in a face to face reference context. The software often allow co-browsing, file sharing, screen capturing and data sharing mining of previous transcripts. Libraries are already offering live reference service using 24x7x265 in a collaborative fashion.

In India, all the Universities and Research Centres have good libraries and most of them are providing web based services. Current Awareness Services (CAS) and Selective Dissemination of Information (SDI) services are being provided to users' community by using web technology at maximum but still few of them are lacking behind due to lack of basic infrastructure and lack of skilled man power. The IITs, IISc, IISERs, NITs, IIMs are the best of them which are providing web based services in true sense. Email is widely used for providing web based services such as new arrivals of books, recent arrivals of print journals, updation to Library web page, new e-resources, Inter-Library Loan etc. Web-OPAC is quite popular among user communities in academic institutions. The launching of INFLIBNET Centre,

Ahmedabad by the UGC in the late eighties has opened up new vistas in the organization of academic and research libraries in India. Presently INFLIBNET is involved in creating infrastructure for sharing of library and information resources and services among Academic and Research Institutions.

MOBILE APPLICATION IN INFORMATION AND LIBRARY SERVICES

Information Technology (IT) consists of all technical means used to handle information and aid communication, including computer and network hardware, communication middleware as well as necessary software. In other words, IT consists of IT as well as telephony, broadcast media, all types of audio and video processing and transmission and network based control and monitoring functions, electronic capturing, processing, storing and disseminating information.The first generation (1G) standard for voice was developed in 1979. This was followed by the second generation (2G) standard using global systems for mobile communications in 1992. The most recent standard that followed is called 3rd Generation (3G). 3rd Generation networks are fully operated in many countries across the world. The 3G technology is developed based on the convergence of different devices, networks and content. The 3G telephone enables users to access data, voice, and video, as well as internet access through wireless application protocol (WAP). The 3G uses the wideband code division multiple access (WCDMA) technique, which is basically a high speed 3G mobile wireless technology with the capacity to offer higher data speeds. WCDMA can reach speeds of up to 2Mbps for voice, video, data and image transmission. Once the 3G technology is introduced, the users can enjoy internet access with a much faster speed using their 3G mobile phone units. Among the services currently available includes traffic monitoring system, instant video clips, live media, "face-to-face" conversation, etc., where all of which are made possible through higher bandwidths.

India as an emerging destination of knowledge economy is getting widely recognized as a global hub for education and trade. Globalisation of innovation and groundbreaking technologies are providing easier access to information resources in enriching the learning experience. Unlike the past, the phenomenal growth of information and communication technology (ICT) has impacted tremendously and the world is rapidly shrinking as the learning communities are brought closer.

From computers to the Internet, libraries have successfully met the challenge of adapting their services to changing technologies. Today's challenge is delivering services to smart phones, eBook readers, and tablets to users. Mobile Technology has now come up with "Libraries in Hand" trend. Our librarians are in move to determine how these devices are affecting information access and ensure that they are communicating with patrons and providing web content in the most appropriate and effective ways. Our Librarians must be prepared to take this challenge and put his efforts to increase the market and demand for mobile access to personalized facts and information anytime, anywhere on one's own handheld device. Since Mobile handled devices truly are personal devices, search histories and physical locations can be harnessed to produce more accurate, individualized information and services. Libraries today are covering most of the technologies given by mobile industry like PDA's, Blackberry, iPod, Cell phones, and mobilizing library contents in a portable form suit able for small screen and delivering short services in the form of contents/ information with device's multiple searching features. Librarians will need to become proficient in using these devices to enable users to access them anywhere from anyplace. Mobile technology has the potential to offer many new possibilities for accessing information from online catalogues, online databases, the internet and virtual libraries. Among the wireless technologies includes digital cellular technologies, packet radio and wireless local area networks. Today, the convergence of mobile phones and the internet through the WAP standard presents libraries with a real opportunity to deploy wireless phone technology to manage their operations for the following services: checking records of books borrowed; alerts on overdue books; alerts on outstanding fines; reminders to return library items; renewing library items; reference enquiry services; text alerts to new resources; alert on library event information; library OPAC/database; Contacting librarian for help.

Mobile application in library services can be established through an infrastructure that integrates the library systems and databases, through an application system that allows for information to be processed and delivered to a smaller device such as a mobile phone unit (Lee, 2007).

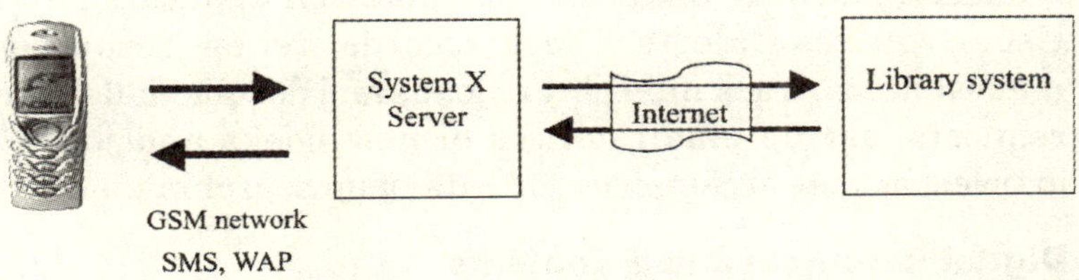

The above figure is an example of a general infrastructure for a possibility of a wireless service that can be provided by the library. The librarians and the library users may take the initiative to liaise with mobile phone service providers, Internet service providers, telecommunication experts and library systems developers to determine how mobile phones can be used to automate library procedures. Major library services are as follows:

SMS NOTIFICATION

Text message alerts provide busy mobile owners with quick news announcements, reminders about important events, or requested information. Libraries can offer these speedy advisories as an added service to patrons. It provides the latest news and notices and reaches users wherever they might be via SMS and MMS from libraries. Users can get notified instantly with notice alerts: alerts on overdue books, outstanding fines, reminders to return library items, library event information, etc. (Herman, 2007).

Access Library Resources

It helps to accesses a variety of library-owned resources and databases. Users can just enter search terms and see results that are designed specifically for mobile viewing. This service includes OPAC (online public access catalogue), integrated search, and original document search.

Personalize Library Services

It provides the following services such as lending extension/inquiry, return information/inquiry, interlibrary loan requests, SDI service application, email service of academic journals, database use education application, etc. Users can read alerts, check records, renew resources, request items, track interlibrary loans and document delivery requests, set up email notices of new books and journal articles, set up preferences for catalogue searching, etc.

Digital Resources and e-Contents

It offers access to a variety of databases and digital resources such as e-Books, e-Journals, Web databases, dissertations, and article databases. Users can get fast relevant answers whenever needed with e-Contents Search, search designed just for mobile user.

Library Guide

It gives users the best of library guide information such as library use guide, question answering service, and library statistics delivering rich content in away that works best for users. If users have questions and want to contact the librarian for help, they can get a fast response from the library via the mobile device and find the appropriate information needed.

FUTURE APPLICATION OF MOBILE IN LIBRARY SERVICES

Library services have changed with the transformations in computing and networking. Mobile technology is necessary to diversify library services for individual needs and an essential solution for anyone. It needs to develop more specialized services such as a customized information service for individual users, more accessibility through ubiquitous environments, and collaboration among organizations. It needs fast, efficient and flexible services to meet the external demands and challenges of today's ubiquitous environment. The expectations of users are increasing at the same or faster rate as information and communication innovations are being developed in the future library. It must first consider which services will be more suitable for the mobile environment and continually seek to identify its role in contributing to social outcomes and objectives in the library field. The following are some issues and challenges related to the further improvement and work in mobile library service.

WIRELESS NETWORKING

Real-time service

Although a variety of library services have been made available over the Internet, mobile library applications allow real-time, anywhere, anytime connectivity to services. Real-time service gives a user anytime, anywhere access to the familiar online content and services users know and trust right from the user's mobile device (Farkas et al. 2006). It helps users instantly get where they want to go in the mobile library, send e-mail, upload reports, download files, search for answers, check notices, or get news. All this and much more are available through realtime service and a mobile device. It will include not only search engines and directory services but also a great variety of information services. Operators have to put extra efforts in identifying and partnering with new concepts and technology to develop personalized real-time services.

Location service

Location service is an information service which provides location-specific information to mobile users and resources moving from location to location. In museum multimedia systems, location information is typically used on one hand to aid navigation, and on the other hand to show information about the exhibits nearby. Searching books in large libraries can be a difficult task for library users. In libraries, users are in different environments and are typically searching for particular resources concerning certain topics. The problem is how to locate the target resources from the numerous shelves of the library. It also broadens the range of service by combining current services and convergence of new telecommunication and broadcasting technology. Operators also plan to enhance user convenience and facilitate service by developing new models that combine current library service with technical services such as RFID, mobile networks, mobile devices, etc. For example, SmartLibrary provides map based guidance to books and collections on a PDA (Aittola et al. 2004).

Personal service

Personalization and customization typically involves presenting users with services that depend on personal characteristics, current location, activity, and surrounding environment (Lee 2007). Personal service allows users to collect all favourite parts of mobile library service in one place. Personal service is typically used to reflect personal interests, provide new information, alert users of services according to their chosen profile, and to collect the user's favourite content in one place. It needs to transfer information quickly or transmit personalized information, etc. It must take more active steps to provide a specialized service different from wired Internet's services in the future and attempt to individualize user service using methods such as My Library, RSS (really simple syndication), etc. My Library supports a framework for libraries to provide enhanced access to local and remote sets of information and knowledge. RSS provides Web contents or summary Web contents together with links to the full content and other metadata (Kajewski 2007).

Multimedia service

Multimedia include a combination of text, audio, still images, animation, video, etc. Compared to existing wireless Internet services that are typically limited to SMS and small amounts of information, operators should plan to provide multimedia-based services to meet user needs by addressing a variety of scenarios that reflect the user's pattern and sensitivity (Bartolomeo 2006). Currently the most common mobile devices are not smart phones or PDAs, but cellular phones or other devices that utilize dial pads. Not only does the limited size of the LCD screen prevent presentation of large amounts of information, but the devices' input system also presents difficulty.

Mobile service

The current goal of mobile service is to enable all services currently provided through wired Internet to be available through mobile networks and to overcome the limitations of current wireless Internet service (Crawford 2006). Operators must analyze the processes of the library services being used by users and the patterns needed in a mobile environment. Then, they must look into gathering innovative information for the application and improvement of mobile library service. They also plan to enhance user convenience and integrate possible services by developing new models that combine current library service with new technology and convergence services. This transcends the traditional sense of the library into an environment where library business can be handled anytime, anywhere. Through the advancements in mobile Internet services, expansion of these new business approaches is being accelerated. Many projects have also launched mobile friendly versions.

Mobile content

Mobile content is any type of media viewed or used on mobile devices (Sugai 2007). It can be categorized by three areas according to the content of information, such as communication (SMS, e-mail, chatting, community, etc), information (ebook, e-learning, shopping, news, notices, location, etc.), and entertainment (ringtone, VOD, game, music, movie, TV, etc.). It is designed for usage at mobile terminals, especially cellular phones and PDAs. Creating and handling mobile content efficiently needs various techniques due to the limitation of resources, such as processing power, memory and communication bandwidth, and available mobile terminals. Although library content has been made available over the wired Internet and library, access from the various mobile devices may not be as widespread as access to wired library service. Various research activities have been launched to develop techniques to implement tools and applications. A mobile library also needs to develop a mobile portal that will provide convenient and useful services to users. This will meet various user needs by accommodating and providing high quality external content along with those developed by libraries. In this perspective, libraries would expect to gain great popularity with personalized multimedia contents such as interactive video, music, games, and learning.

Mobile technology convergence

The convergence of telecommunications and broadcasting is expected to become a widespread phenomenon in the future (Shin 2006). This convergence of technology has significant impact on the design of future library infrastructures. In order to provide an effective convergence service combining wireless data and multimedia services, various solutions based on the terminal framework that can ensure user convenience must be secured and terminals that can converge with other high-tech industries must be developed simultaneously. Communication and collaboration between Internet, mobile, media, and library will be a top issue over the next few years due to the technology convergence explosion. Indian libraries need to be indispensable to their users, and to this end they have to include mobile devices as part of their strategic thinking. Mobile libraries have to grow, and this requires greater collaboration between academic, industry, corporations and government. In the current scenario, mobile libraries have the potential to proliferate and we will witness a situation in which the mobile will definitely be used as a tool to spread learning across the country.

Advancements in data transmission rates and device design have greatly improved the mobile internet browsing experience. Newer products such as the iPhone, the iPod Touch, most modern BlackBerrys, such as the Bold or the Storm models, and the Palm Pre have integrated the easy downloading, storing and viewing of PDF documents and Microsoft Office files for word processing and spreadsheet formats. These recent enhancements suggest that future developments and previously mentioned demographic patterns will enable a large number of library users to easily use many of these library services from handheld mobile computing devices. Furthermore, these devices are increasingly able to connect to the internet using Wi-Fi connections when available as opposed to using slower and often expensive cell phone connections. Trend towards faster and more ubiquitous internet access will only continue with the development of new technologies, such as Worldwide Inter-operability for Microwave Access (Wimax) or 4G systems . The progress of mobile technologies on wireless networks has largely changed the way people access information. A mobile library is one area being actively explored by many libraries to support remote users in their access to and use of library resources. The widespread use of cellular phones and mobile devices might have also led to the positive opinion and perception on their application in the library services. Mobile technology has the potential to offer many new possibilities for accessing information from online catalogues, databases, digital content, e-learning, digital library, etc. The development and application of new mobile technologies has brought about many changes and possibilities and encourages users to increase utilization of the new mobile library. While these new devices and data transmission technologies are able to bring the mobile internet experience closer to the level of a large screen web browsing experience, it is likely that there will remain differences in how the internet is used on handheld mobile devices.

Mobile service, compared to wired Internet service, has relatively slow transmission speed, limited computational power, inconvenient input and output interface, insufficient contents, and high price. However, it also offers portability of information use, convenience, and speed. A variety of fields utilize wireless mobile technology for these advantages in order to increase business productivity and efficiency. Technology improvement will provide users to obtain relevant information more easily and freely, and the library will actively study and develop new service models to meet those needs continuously. The further development of emerging technology and new technology convergence will provide the ubiquitous library with new innovative ways of delivering its information resources, services, and instructions. It is impossible to anticipate all new technologies. There is clear recognition that mobile technologies and devices are experiencing very high adoption rates in many regions of the world. The current trend shows that among the various models of mobile library being adopted, the cooperative model is increasingly popular.

LIBRARY IN THE CLOUD

Cloud technology is a set of network devices designed specifically for the storage and transmissions of a great variety of data. All devices are synchronized with up to date content at any time. Cloud technology allows users to store their work files on cloud servers, which can then be edited from any computer with an internet connection. Innovation changes technology and technology changes the mode of service. Cloud technology is currently changing the way we read, store and transfer data, including the modes of interaction with library services. Cloud technology is a revolutionary initiative that will bring disruptive changes to the library. In general cloud technology is more suitable for mobile devices. Mobile phones and pads have been limited in terms of storage and processing capacity. Some of the storage and processing loads may then be relegated to the cloud servers. But such limitations are currently being overcome on high end devices. More important is the fact that cloud technology support ubiquitous computing using mobile devices. Cloud technology has thus changed the mobile phone, from communications equipment into a handheld device connected to the network. Such functionality is also a challenge for the library field.

By using cloud technology, libraries and especially the smaller ones no longer need to configure complex computer system and other infrastructure for themselves. They can get rid of physical equipment and its technical constraints and drop the burden of software maintenance. Instead they can focus more on library's original tasks: services and innovation. Library resources may be distributed in the cloud, with global mobile access, to really achieve a global library network. Using cloud technology, sharing library resources global-a simultaneous happening is becoming true. The basic usage of "cloud" is to store and to share. Data are stored in the cloud servers, that anybody free to use on any kinds of devices at anytime, anywhere. This is exactly consistent with digital libraries' vision.

REFERENCES

Aittola, M., P. Parhi, M. Vieruaho, and T. Ojala. 2004. Comparison of mobile and fixed use of SmartLibrary. Proc. 6th International Conference on Human Computer Interaction with Mobile Devices and Services, Glasgow, Scotland : 383–387.

Akeroyd, J. (1991) 'Launch of CD network has rapid impact', *Information World Review,* 59, pp.10-11.

Arant, W. and Payne, L. (2001) 'The common user interface in academic libraries: myth or reality?' *Library Hi- Tech,* 19: 1, pp. 63–76.

Arora, J. (2003) 'Indian national digital library in engineering science and technology (INDEST): a proposal for strategic cooperation for consortia-based access to electronic resources', *International Information & Library Review,* 35, pp.1-17.

Badu, E. E. (1993) 'The impact of the use of microcomputers on the university of Ghana Library', *Library Review,* 42: 5, pp. 23- 37.

Bansode, S. and Pujar, S.M. (2008) 'Scholarly Digital Library Initiatives: World Versus India' *DESIDOC Journal of Library & Information Technology,* 28: 6, pp. 21-26.

Bartolomeo, G. et al. 2006. SMS: Simplifying mobile services – for users and service providers. Telecommunications, 2006. AICTICIW '06. International conference on Internet and web applications and services/advanced international conference: 209 –214.

Bavakutty, M. and Majeed, Abdul (2005) *Methods for Measuring Quality of Libraries,* New Delhi: Ess Ess Publications, 2005.

Bichteler, J. (1987) 'Techno stress in libraries: Causes, effects and solutions', *The Electronic Library,* 5: 5, pp. 1-3.

Biddiscombe, R. (1991) 'Networking CD-ROMs at the university of Birmingham library', *ITs News,* 24, pp. 27-28.

Borgman, C. (1997) 'From acting locally to thinking globally: a brief history of library automation', *The Library Quarterly,* 67: July, pp. 215-249.

Breeding, M. (2005) 'Looking towards the future of library technology', *Computers in Libraries: Library Technology Guides,* 25: 25, pp.1-5.

Broadbent, Marianne & Lofgren, Hans (1991). *Priorities, Performance and Benefits: An Exploratory Study of Library and Information Units.* Melbourne, Centre for International Research on Communication and Information Technologies & Australian Council of Libraries and Information Services.

Budd, J. M. and Connaway, L. S. (1997) 'University faculty and networked information: results of a survey', *Journal of the American Society for Information Science,* 48: 9, pp.843-852.

Cairncross, F. (1997) *The Dearth of the Distance,* Boston, Harvard Business School.

Carnegie, Garry D and West, Brian P (2003) "Placing Monetary Values on Public Repositories of Knowledge: Why, When, How and So What?" Paper presented at the Council of Australian University Librarian Seminar, Cairns, Australia.

Caver, B. (2003) 'Is it time to get blogging?' Available from http://proquest.umi.com/

Chopra, Y. L. and Mukherjee, B. (2000) 'Application of IT in university library services of Jabalpur (Madhya Pradesh State)', *Annals of Library Science and Documentation,* 47 : 2, pp.49–51.

Clyde, L. A. (2004) 'Weblogs – are you serious?' *The Electronic Library,* 22: 5, pp.390-402.

Cohan, M. J., Kelsey, A. L. and Ficls, K. M. (1998) *Planning for Library Automation: a Practical Hand Book,* London, Library Association Pub.

Cortez. E. M. (1983) 'Library automation and management information systems', *Journal of Library Administration,* 4: 3, pp. 21-33.

Crawford, D. I. 2006. Spectrum for mobile multimedia services. Consumer electronics, ISCE '06. 2006 IEEE tenth international symposium: 1–4.

Daniels. R. I. (1995) 'Effects on non-professional staff of the implementation of computer-based library systems in college libraries: some case studies', *Program,* 29: 1, pp.1-13.

Dawson, P. and Palmer, Gill (1995). *Quality Management: the Theory and Practice of Implementing Change.* Longman, Melbourne.

Debrowski, D. S. (1999) 'Library technicians and the management of technology innovation, projection/reflections: our heritage and our future 2000 and beyond' in Proceedings of 10th ALIA National Library Technicians Conference, Perth, Australian Library and Information Association (ALIA).

DELNET (2011) 'About Ourselves', Available from http://www.delnet.nic.in/about-ourselves.htm

Dobb, L. S. (1999), 'Four retreats and a forum: a meditation on retreats as a response to change', *Library Trends,* 47: 4, pp.699-710.

Doug, G. and Vogel, T. M. (2003) 'Building a Home for Library News with a Blog', Available from http://proquest.umi.com/

Dyer, H., Fossey, D. and McKee, K. (1993) 'The impact of automated library systems on job design and staffing structures', *Program,* 27: 1, pp. 1-16.

Evans, P. (2000) 'E-lending: the next wave to hit libraries?' *Biblio Tech Review: Information Technology for Libraries Review*, January 28.

Farkas, K. et al. 2006. Real-time service provisioning for mobile and wireless networks. Computer Communications 29: 540 –550.

Fecko, M. B. (1997) *Electronic Resources: Access and Issues,* London, Bowker.

Frey, T. (2005) *The Future of Libraries Beginning the Great Transformation*, Colorado, The DaVinci Institute, Inc.

Furuta, K. (1990) 'The Impact of automation on professional catalogers', *Information Technology and Libraries,* September, pp. 242-252.

Ganpule. S. R and Waydande, H. S. (1991) 'Computerisation and aftermath in central library of IIT Bombay', Paper presented in the seminar on library automation and it after math, 5-6, April, Hyderabad, ASRC.

Groenewegen, Hans, Lim, Edward (1995). TQM and Quality Assurance at Monash University Library. *AARL Australian Academic and Research Libraries* 26, 6-16.

Hane, P. J. (2001) 'Blogs are a natural for librarians', (online). Available from http://www.infotoday.com/newslink/newslink0110.htm

Haravu, L. J. (1995) 'Strategies for tile adoption of new information technologies in Indian libraries', *paper presented in CALIBER-95: National Convention on Information access through networks,* 10-12, February, Hyderabad.

Harbour, R. T. (1994) *Managing library automation,* London, ASLIB.

Harder, G. and Reichardt, R. (2003) Throw another Blog on the Wire: Libraries and the Blogging Phenomenon. Felicciter 2.

Hauptman, R. and Anderson, C. L. (1994) 'The people speak: the dispersion and impact of technology in American libraries', *Information Technology and Libraries,* 13: 4, pp.249-256.

Herman, Sonia. 2007. SMS reference: keeping up with your clients. The Electronic Library 25(4): 401 –408.

Hernon, P., Nitecki, D., Altman, E. (1999). Service Quality and Customer Satisfaction: An Assessment and Future Directions. *Journal of Academic Librarianship* 25, 9-17.

Hernon, Peter and Whitman, John R. (2001). *Delivering Satisfaction and Service Quality: A Customer-Based Approach for Libraries.* American Library Association, Chicago.

Heskett, James L. et.al. (1997). *The Service Profit Chain.* Free Press, New York.

Hirnmelfarb, G. (1999) 'Revolution in the library', *Library Trends,* 47: 4, pp. 612-619.

Hisle, L. W. (2002) 'Top issues facing academic libraries: a report of the focus on the future task force', *C&RL News,* 63: 10, pp. 1-3.

Hofmann, U. (1995) 'Developing a strategic planning framework for information technologies for libraries', OCLC systems and services, II: 4, pp. 22-32.

Horny, K. L. (1987) 'Fifteen years of automation: evolution of technical services staffing', *Library Resources and Technical Services,* 310, pp. 69-76.

Hyde, J. (1997) 'How soon is now? Current developments and future possibilities for libraries and librarians: a library technician's view', *The Australian Library journal,* 46: May, pp.181-185.

Johnson, P. (1991) *Automation and organizational change in libraries, Boston,* G.K. Hall.

Kajewski, Mary Ann. 2007. Emerging technologies changing our service delivery models. The Electronic Library 25(4): 420 –429.

Kannappanavar, B. U. and Vijayakumar, M. (2001) 'Use of IT in university of agricultural science libraries of Karnataka: a comparative study', *DESIDOC Bulletin of Information Technology,* 21:1, pp.21–26.

Karami, T. and Oloumi, T. (2006) 'Libraries and Weblogs: the Role of new phenomenon Blogs in library services research and learning', *paper presented at the twenty seventh Annual Conference on Embedding Libraries in Learning and Research,* 22-25, May, Faculdade De Engenharia, Porto, Portugal, International Association of Technological University Libraries (IATUL).

Karim, N. S. A., Darus, S. H. and Hussin, R. (2006) 'Mobile applications in academic library services: a student's feedback survey, *Campus-Wide information Systems,* 23: 1, pp. 35-51.

Karim, Nor Shahriza Abdul, Siti Hawa Darus, and Ramlah Hussin. 2006. Mobile phone applications in academic library services: a students' feedback survey. Campus-Wide Information Systems 23(1): 35–51.

Kemparaju, T. D. and Nyamboga, C. N. (2001) 'Why IT course in the curriculum of library and information science?' *SELS Journal of Information Management,* 38: 3, pp. 201–210.

Kiesler, S., Obrosky, S. and Pratto, F. (1987) 'Automating a university library: some effects on work and workers' In Kiesler, S. and Sproull, L. (eds), *Computing and change on campus,* Cambridge, Cambridge University Press.

Klein, L. (2005) 'Leo Klein's top technology trends, June 23, 5 pages.

Klerk, A. De and Euster, J. R. (1989) 'Technology and organisation metamorphoses', *Library Trends,* 37: 4, pp.457-468.

Klobas, J. E. (1990) 'Managing technological changes in libraries and information services', *The Electronic Library,* 8: 5, pp.344-349.

Kumar, P. S. G. (1987) *Computerisation of Indian libraries, Delhi,* B.R. Publishing Corporation.

Kumar, R. P. (1993) 'Application of modern technologies in health science libraries in India: a survey', *Aslib Proceedings,* 45: 3, pp.63–67.

Lakos, Amos (2001). Culture of assessment as a catalyst for organizational culture in libraries. In *Meaningful Measures for Emerging Realities: Proceedings of the 4th Northumbria International Conference on performance Measurement in Libraries and Information Services* (J. Stein, M. Kyrillidou, and D. Davis, eds.), pp. 311-319. Association of research Libraries, Washington, DC.

Lee, Wei-Po. 2007. Deploying personalized mobile services in an agent-based environment. Expert Systems with Applications 32(4): 1194 –1207.

Leon, A. and Leon, M. (1998) *Fundamental of computer science and communication engineering,* New Delhi, Vikas Publishing.

Lewis, B. R. (1991) *Managing Service Quality.* In. Managing Quality. New York: Academic Press, p234-235.

Lipctz, Ben-Ami and Paulson, Peter 1. (1987) 'A study of the impact of introducing an online subject catalog at the New York State Library', *Library Trends,* 35, pp.619-629.

Lipow, A. (1999) 'In your face reference service', *Library Journal,* 124: 13, pp. 50-52.

Martinez-Arellano, Filiberto F. (1996) 'User attitudes and behavior before and after the implementation of an On-line Catalog', *International Information & Library Review,* 28, pp.275-287.

Matthews, J. R. (1986) *The Impact of Online Catalogs*, New York, Neal-Schuman.

Matthews, J. R., Lawrence, G. S. and Ferguson, D. K. (1983) *Using Online Catalogs: A Nationwide Survey*, New York, Neal-Schuman.

Mayer, I. (2002) 'Using text messaging to improve student organization and motivation', Available from http://ferl.becta.org.uk/

Mc Donald, D. R. (1984) *Planning the Integrated Library System: A discursion paper for cabinet*, University of Michigan Library System Office, Arm Arbor.

McGregor, F. (2004) *Excellent Libraries: A Quality Assurance Perspective*, in Niteki, DA (ed), Advances in Librarianship, 28, 17-53.

McGregor, Felicity (1997). Quality assessment - combating complacency. *Australian Library Journal*, 46, 82-92.

McGregor, Felicity (2000). Performance Measures, Benchmarking and Value. In *ALIA 2000 Capitalising on knowledge the information profession in the 21st century: Proceedings*, ALIA, Canberra.

McGregor, Felicity (2001). "Inside, outside and upside down"'. Paper presented at the International Business Excellence Summit, 25-27 March, Sydney Convention and Exhibition Centre, Darling Harbour.

McGregor, Felicity (2003) "Benchmarking with the Best." Paper presented at the 5th Northumbria International Conference on Performance Measurement in Libraries and Information Services, Durham, England.

McMenemy, D. and Poulter, A. (2005) *Delivering Digital Services: Handbook for Public libraries and Learning Centres*. London: Facet Publishing.

Mfrisque (2006) 'Core competencies in Library technology: what IT is and where IT is going', Available from http://litablog.org/.

Morgan, E. (2006) 'Eric Lease Morgan's Top Tech Trends for ALA 2006: Some Pontifications', Available from http://litablog.org/

Mujoo-Munish and Virmalhan (1998) 'Information technology: concerns and issues in developing countries with special reference to India', *Library Herald*, 36: 2, pp.69

O'Leary, M. (1990) 'Local online: the genie is out of the bottle', *Online*, 14: 1, pp.15-18.

Orenstein, D. (2006) 'Trends in the library profession and the impact of technology at the Montgomery College Libraries', (online). Available from http://www.mjfredman.org/

Pathak, S.K., Mishra, A. and Sahoo, G. (2008) 'Future of Web Based Library And Information Servicess: An Indian Scenario', *PLANNER – 2008*, INFLIBNET, pp.406-414

Pease. S. and Gouke, M. I. (1982) 'Patterns of use in an online catalog and a card catalog', *College and Research Libraries,* 43, pp. 279-291.

Pong, L. Y. (1990) 'Computerisation of library operations in Singapore: an overview', *International Library Review,* 22, pp.163-179.

Prince, B. and Burton, P. F. (1988) 'Changing dimensions in academic library structures: the impact of information technology', *British Journal of Academic Librarianship,* 3: 2, pp.67-81.

Quinn, Brian (1997). Adapting service quality concepts to academic libraries. *Journal of Academic Librarianship* 23, 359-369.

Raina, Roshan (1999) *Total Quality Management in Library and Information Services.* New Delhi: Infuse Inc,p1-151.

Ramos, M. and Piper, P. S. (2006) 'Letting the grass grow: grassroots information on Blogs and Wikis', Reference Services Review. 34: 4, pp. 570-574.

Ranganathan, S. R. (1988) *Five Laws of Library Science,* Ed.2. Bangalore: SRELS.

Rao, I. K. R. (1997) 'Automation of academic libraries in India: status, problems and future (Theme Paper) in CAL1BER-1997: Information Technology Applications on Academic Libraries', *Papers presented at the Fourth National Convention for the automation of libraries in education and research.* 6-8, March, (pp. I-4). Ahmedabad: INFLIBNET Centre.

Rao, I. K. R. (1983) 'Library automation', *paper presented at DRTC refresher seminar,* Bangalore.

Rao, S. S. (2001) 'Networking of libraries and information centres: challenges in India'. *Library HI TECH,* 19: 2, PP. 167–178.

Ressler, S. and Trefzger, B. (1997) 'Development of the NIST virtual library', IEEE *internet computing, Sep*/Oct, pp. 35-41.

Rowley, J. E. (1993). *Computers for libraries,* 3 (Rev. Ed.), London, Library Association Publishing

Saurine, K. (2000) 'Head in the Clouds...feet on the ground', *The Australian Library Journal,* 49: 1, pp.65-71.

Schatz, B. and Chen, H. (1999) 'Digital libraries: technological Advances and social impacts', *IEEE Computer*, 32: 2, pp.45-50.

Sharma, Pandey S. K. (1993) 'Library computerisation: why Information Technology and Librarianship', *papers presented at AGLIS Annual National Convention*, Jaipur.

Shaughnessy, T.W. (1995). Total Quality Management: It's Application in North American Research Libraries. *AARL Australian Academic and Research Libraries* 26, 1-5.

Shaw, D. (1986) 'Staff opinions in library automation planning: a case study', *Special libraries,* 77: 3, pp.140-151.

Shin, Dong-Hee. 2006. Convergence of telecommunications, media and information technology, and implications for regulation. Info 8(1): 42 –56.

Sierpe, E. (2004) "Managing the information revolution: library management, the control of perspective technologies, and the future of librarianship, *Library Management,* 25: 4/5, pp.177-182.

Singh, S. P. (2001) 'Computer applications in Indian institutes of technology libraries', *Electronic Library,* 19 : 2, pp. 92–101.

Sirkin, A.F. (1993). Customer Service: Another Side of TQM. *Journal of Library Administration* 18, 71-83.

Smith, E. D. (1993) 'A comparison of the effects of new technology on searching habits in industrial and academic institutions', *Journal of Information Science,* 19, pp.57-66.

Starkweather, W. M. and Wallin, C. C. (1999) 'Faculty response to library technology: insights on attitudes', *Library Trends,* 47: 4, pp. 640-668.

Steenderen, M. V. (2002) 'Business application of WAP', *The Electronic Library,* 20: 3, pp. 215-223.

Sugai, Philip. 2007. Exploring the impact of handset upgrades on mobile content and service usage. International Journal of Mobile Communications 5(3): 281 –299.

Sun Micro Systems (2003) 'Information Technology Advances in Libraries', Available from http://www.sun.com/edu/

Sykes, P. (1986) 'Automation and non-professional staff at the Polytechnic of the South Bank', *Training and Education,* 3: 3, pp. 50-56.

Tenopir, C. and Ennis, L. (1998) 'The Impact of Digital Reference on Librarians and Library Users', *Online,* 22: 6, pp. 84-86.

Thakuria, Pranjit Kumar (2007) Concept of: An Overview, 5th

Convention Planner-2007, Gauhati University, Guwahati, December 7-8, 2007 INFLIBNET Centre, Ahmedabad.

Wright, K. C. (1995) *Computer- related technologies in library operation,* England, Gower.

Yaacob R. A. and Harun, M. H. (1996) 'Information technology implementations in libraries and information centres in Malaysia: impact and pitfalls', *Electronic Library* 14: 3, pp. 233-242.